RE-MEMBERING GOD

Re·membering God

Human Hope and Divine Desire

TOBIAS STANISLAS HALLER BSG

Copyright © 2019 by Tobias Stanislas Haller BSG
Images copyright © by Tobias Stanislas Haller BSG

All rights reserved. No part of this book may be reproduced, stored in a retrieval system, or transmitted in any form or by any means, electronic or mechanical, including photocopying, recording, or otherwise, without the written permission of the publisher.

Unless otherwise noted, the scripture quotations contained herein are from the New Revised Standard Version Bible, copyright © 1989 by the Division of Christian Education of the National Council of Churches of Christ in the U.S.A. Used by permission. All rights reserved.

Church Publishing
19 East 34th Street
New York, NY 10016
www.churchpublishing.org

Cover art: "Christ Enthroned," Tempera on board, 2003, Tobias Stanislas Haller BSG
Cover design by Jennifer Kopec, 2Pug Design
Typeset by PerfecType, Nashville, Tennessee

A record of this book is available from the Library of Congress.

ISBN-13: 978-1-64065-152-4 (pbk.)
ISBN-13: 978-1-64065-153-1 (ebook)

Remember, remember,
Come home, my scattered children!
Here's bread to break
    and wine to drink.
Sit down and eat,
and I will wash your feet.
Remember, remember—
Sit still, my noisy children!
I'll speak the prayer
    and sing the song
that tells of glory.
Listen to the story.
Remember, remember?
Look at my hands, my children,
Look at my side:
I am your friend
    no longer dead
but known in broken bread.
—*Anamnesis,* 1997

Contents

0. Introduction: The Church and Its Foundation. 1
1. The Hand and the Jawbone: The Dominion of Text. 5
2. Ascetics and Aesthetics: The Trinity Whom We Adore 19
3. The Lost Coin: Human Roles and Divine Images. 29
4. Behold Who You Are: The Icon as Sacrament of
   God's Presence. 51
5. The Spirit at Work in Church and World 63
6. When in Our Music: Feathers on the Breath of God 75
7. The Stones Themselves Shall Sing: Architecture for Glory. . . . 87
8. Turned Toward Mission: People Look East 99
9. Known in Bread: The Eucharist at the Heart of Worship . . . 113
10. The Day Thou Givest: The Daily Office as Cosmic Dance. . . 119
11. Why We Pray: Prayer as Praxis, Praxis as Prayer. 129
12. The Knowledge and the Love of God: Limits of Our
    Quest, Extent of Our Song 143
13. Teach Us to Pray: The Lord's Prayer as Microcosmic
    Re-creation 149
References and Acknowledgments 171

Introduction

The Church and Its Foundation

First, another poem:

> The tall old priest entered the half-lit sacristy,
> fresh from his usual Tuesday morning studies.
> The fair-haired acolyte with the bad complexion
> was ready, vested, standing in the dimness
> quietly. The old priest noticed he was sniffing
> and his eyes were red. A failed romance,
> he thought; but keeping his own rule on chit-chat
> in the sacristy, vested silently.
> The old familiar motions and the prayers
> displaced whatever thoughts he might have had;
> the only dialogue to break the stillness was
> the rote exchange of formal preparation.
> Then, in one motion as he slipped his hand
> beneath the pale green veil, the other hand
> upon the burse, he lifted vested vessels,
> turned and followed in the sniffing server's
> wake. Eyes lowered to the holy burden
> in his hand, he failed to notice that
> the chapel for this midday feria—
> on other days like this with one or two

> at most—was full of worshipers; until
> he raised his eyes, and saw the pews were filled—
> but undeterred began the liturgy:
> the lessons and the gospel from last Sunday,
> his sermon brief, but pointed, on the texts.
> It wasn't till the acolyte began
> the people's prayers, and choked out words of planes
> that brought a city's towers down, and crashed
> into the Pentagon, and plowed a field
> in Pennsylvania, that the old priest knew
> this was no ordinary Tuesday in
> September—
> > not ordinary time at all,
> that day he missed the towers' fall.
> —*September Midday Mass,* 2008

It was only a few short weeks after a tragic weekday in September that I flew—one of a handful of passengers—to Wisconsin to lead a long-planned retreat for the brothers and sisters of the Order of Julian of Norwich. It was to be a silent week, apart from the words of the office and the mass, and the meditations I would offer day by day. Coming as I did from the horrors just endured in New York, I appreciated the time for quiet, for prayer, for reflection. Some of what follows in this volume either formed or grew out of that experience of recovery amidst the ruins.

The heart of the matter is how the church functions, with God, in putting together the broken pieces of our lives, the scattered fragments of our world, and of the church itself, the divided and wounded body of Christ. In this work, our human hopes mesh with the desire of God for wholeness and restoration. As the poem suggests, the church—in the person of the priest who performs a day-to-day routine of prayer and worship—may not even be aware of its role. At the same time, the church—in the persons of the assembly who turn out and turn up, some of them only when and as tragedy strikes—keenly discerns where to find help in time of need, for sorrow or rejoicing, the two or three gathered constituting the real presence of Christ with, in, and through them.

Introduction

Anglicans have long held that the church, being made of such fallible people as these, as us, is itself fallible. The church is, as one traditional prayer puts it, a wonderful and sacred mystery, but there are things about it that have been cast down and grown old, things that are in need of being raised and renewed. This book looks to some of these aspects of the church, hoping with human hope for the raising and renewal that God desires and promises. These are aspects of form and content, word and action (or as the liturgists would say, rite and ceremony), prayer and petition, doing and being. Some of them have indeed grown old, dating from the earliest days of the church. Some have been neglected or forgotten, or seldom used, so old that when they reappear some mistake them for novelties; other means of liturgical prayer are shopworn through their overuse, and through familiarity have almost lost their power to startle and convict. We need constant reminders that there is no "ordinary time" when time is touched by human pain or joy or hope, or by divine desire.

The human hope and divine desire is that all of these moments and means can be, as the old prayer says, brought to their perfection by the one through whom all things were made. That Living One continues to act through the very imperfect members of the church, the body of Christ, which like our own bodies continues to live even as the individual members of which it is made up pass out of life, from what used to be called the church militant into the church expectant or triumphant.

The human might well ask how the imperfect and transitory can hope to come to eternal perfection, however much the divine desires it. The human has been faced with such questions before, as in, "Can these dry bones live again?" and "Can anything good come out of Nazareth?" It is God who works in, through, and with the transitory imperfect, bringing it to a higher order of eternal perfection than it can ever attain on its own. It is the human hope to collaborate in this divine endeavor, with God supplying the strength and correcting the errors, to re-member the body of God shaped to the perfection of divine desire.

What follows are essays about that hope and endeavor, some reminders to re-member. Some may find that a few of these are Episcopal "inside baseball" or majoring in the minors. My response is twofold.

The Episcopal Church is the one in which I minister, and I trust that no ministry ends at the church door or the boundaries of a parish or a diocese. Secondly, nothing is too small or too fleeting in God's sight. The God whom we worship and adore is particularly concerned with the small and short-lived, with sparrows and field flowers. The Episcopal Church may be small among the Christian bodies; even the Anglican Communion as a whole cannot compete in sheer numbers with some of its larger Christian cousins. Small as we are, and as trifling as some of our liturgical, devotional, and spiritual practices may seem, I trust that God works in and through these seemingly less important or rejected members, here treated with honor and care, re-membered into place, perhaps surprisingly discovered to be cornerstones after all.

The Hand and the Jawbone

The Dominion of Text

Prelude

My friend Peter entered into Christ through a little blue door.

He came to Columbia University in the waning years of the sixties as a freshly minted graduate student, plagued with the usual doubts and goaded by the usual hopes of young men of that age and time and place. God was, as everyone knew, dead—or at least not feeling very well—but the church as an institution still seemed to have some utility. Indeed, the civil rights struggle had shown the church to be one of the few things still alive and kicking against a world whose heart seemed to have grown cold.

Peter was drawn to the church by a fierce and uncompromising intellect, a passion for justice and civil rights, and a cultured taste in art and music. He wanted to learn more about the church before he got too deeply involved, however; to talk with those in the know about such things, to learn more, before becoming too enmeshed, about this *religion*.

And so he called on his neighborhood parish church, which happened to be that big, unfinished hulk on Morningside Heights, the Cathedral Church of Saint John the Divine. Apart from the shell of

Coventry, Saint John's is perhaps the most eloquent metaphor for the church in stone—not quite cast down though not completely raised up and definitely grown old in the process of its extended incompletion. Given Peter's intellect, passion for civil rights, and refined taste in things aesthetic, the fact that this was the *Episcopal* cathedral no doubt added its own glimmer of hope. The Episcopal Church was considered by many to be "the thinking person's church" and had taken a moderate but positive stand on matters of social justice. And even in the fading glow of the Episcopal Church's golden years (in which it had been purported to have the corner on good taste), while some Episcopalians were experimenting with colored felt banners and guitars, Saint John the Divine *was* still the church of Louis Comfort Tiffany and Ralph Adams Cram.

In response to Peter's call, he received the name of Canon Edward Nason West, who would be, the receptionist thought, the best person to answer his questions. When Peter phoned him, Canon West, in a flurry of impatience, said he was much, much too busy to see him that week, but if he would come to such-and-such a place ("It's a little blue door about halfway up the cathedral on the southern side, my dear") at 10:45 next Sunday morning, he might have some time to answer his questions about religion.

Peter, with the innocence of youth and the limitations of a culture that has forgotten what happens in cathedrals at about that time on a Sunday, went through the little blue door into that hushed and cavernous space—and why is it that churches always look so much bigger on the inside?—and asked for Canon West. Before he knew what was happening, he was whisked into the sacristy, vested and girded in an oatmeal polyester alb, handed a massive baroque processional crucifix, and placed at the head of a procession, maintained in place by the stern eye, finger snaps, and occasional barked commands of the indomitable Canon West, and by the meaningful nods, gestures, and elbows of his fellow ministers. Peter was simply furious, but he dared not challenge the imposing figure of the canon. Between the shaved head, bushy eyebrows, graying goatee, flowing black vestments, and a wizardish staff, one could not at first glance tell exactly what powers might be at his disposal. *The*

Lord of the Rings had just appeared in paperback, and West looked as if he might have stepped from its pages.

Even had Peter been so inclined or so bold as to challenge him, before he could protest he found himself swept up in the order-in-chaos of a liturgy according to the "Western" Rite as only West could compound it—a superfluity of crosses and streaming embroidered banners emerged from clouds of incense, floating like the masts and sails of antique dream-ships navigating the strange fjords of towering rough-hewn rock columns and walls; the roar of the organ resounded in that cavernous space, individual notes unimportant and unintelligible in the crash and wash of breakers of harmony; ranks of ministers, acolytes, and prelates, in vestments ancient and modern, gloriously colorful, undemocratically heraldic and hierarchic; and there was Peter at the focal point—just behind the man with the jingle-bell thurible swinging and twirling the prayers of the saints up and up into that vaulted dome—there was Peter carrying the huge crucifix down the central aisle, the congregation bowing row by row in waves as he passed, as if pressed down by the power of the weight of glory he was carrying aloft. And all the while he thought, "I'll kill him!"

After the liturgy, as he was hanging up the borrowed alb, still quivering with anger and hurt and disorientation, Canon West came up behind him and laid an authoritative hand upon his shoulder. He spun him around and, peering deeply from beneath a furrowed brow, said, "Now, my boy, I'm prepared to talk to you about our religion."

LITURGICAL PRECEDENCE

In this collection of essays, I am going to be so bold as to talk about our religion. I hope, however, to do so within the context of the sights and sounds and smells and tastes that form the wordless architecture of our sacramental life, the framework of time and space and matter in which the words of prayer are uttered. We will get to words as well, of course, but primarily in the context of movement, light, color, and sound that serves as their setting. I hope to do this in the spirit of what Aidan Kavanagh called "liturgical theology." Kavanagh was a Benedictine and a liturgist: in his person he summarized the theme of re-membering human hopes in line with divine desire, for it is no accident that monastics, and among them especially Benedictines, often make the best and most serious liturgists—after all, they spend much of their time and energy doing what for many Christians (even clergy) is a Sunday morning affair. The Benedictine monks understand a good bit of what they do to be nothing less than *the work of God*. This is a multivalent phrase, and we will pick up on its themes again in this exploration: liturgy is work we do as and for the people of God; it is the "working" of God as God is made present in and through that work; and it is God working in us to God's own glory, realizing God's desires through human hopes expressed and offered.

So it is about that work, the liturgy and worship of the church, and the feelings and thoughts to which it gives rise, that I write. The primary principle of liturgical theology is, as Kavanagh said, "that worship, conceived broadly, is what gives rise to theological reflection, rather than the other way around" (3). Of course, the two are in constant dialogue; belief and liturgy shape each other and are in relationship as form and content. Liturgical forms—especially verbal forms in their urgency to explain and unpack—can sometimes give the impression that the content of the faith is more limited than it actually is; there are truths of faith that cannot be expressed in anything other than sighs and groans too deep for words. This is where liturgical art emerges to begin to try to express the otherwise inexpressible.

So in these pages, we will interrogate our worship and prayer, the who, what, when, where, why, and how of it all, and in particular how it is that seeing, hearing, tasting, smelling, and touching can paradoxically bring us closer to the invisible, unheard, and intangible Reality at the heart of existence.

Kavanagh argued that the church was accustomed to *doing* things before it *explained the significance* of what it was doing, and that as time passed, the secondary explanation came more and more to replace the primary action. Or, as I choose to describe it, the jawbone came to dominate the hand as the most strenuously exercised portion of the church's body—the church's hierarchs (for the most part men, exercising their concept of headship) mansplaining to the bulk of the church's body, the bride of Christ, while she sat patiently keeping her watch and no doubt sighed to herself, "How long . . . ?"

Kavanagh made his argument forcibly, in a number of books and speeches, with the racy, colorful, no-holds-barred, take-no-prisoners style that liturgists have refined through the centuries. It is not difficult for anyone familiar with church history to accept his argument, even were it made less sharply. The earliest evidence we have (the synoptic and 1st Corinthian accounts of the Lord's Supper) shows that the church was in the custom of "doing in remembrance" before explicating the actions and spinning out a secondary eucharistic theology, the scripture itself (particularly Paul's writings) being the first such attempt. One can well suppose that the earliest Eucharists, especially in the solemn moments before the breaking of the bread, may well have been completely silent, without any verbal explanation whatsoever. This would certainly justify Paul's need to supply an "explanation" to the Corinthian converts— telling them that we do these things *because* on the night Jesus suffered *he* did these things. The institution narrative itself, as central as we now hold it to be, may well have originated as a gloss to an action that only lost its eloquence when, to curb the abuses of the Corinthian dinner parties, Paul had to *recall* the congregation to order as the body of Christ: an anamnesis and "discernment of the body" in every sense of those words.

What is true of the Eucharist is also true of the other foundational sacrament. As Kavanagh noted, "Baptism gave rise to the Trinitarian creeds" (92). In the first few centuries, nearly all of the church's theology was, to some extent, a kind of catechumenate before and mystagogy after the experience of the sacraments—building a theological system upon the basis of direct experience of material signs transformed *by* grace into sacraments *for* grace, recalling the church to the fundamental mysteries of creation and redemption, in death-dealing water and life-giving bread. Moreover, as Kavanagh said (18), this secondary theology was largely the work of those who sat in the cathedra rather than in the classroom, people whose jawbone exercise stemmed from (and did not replace) their hands-on experience as pastors and celebrants. In the early church, theology was expounded most often by leaders accustomed to presiding at and participating in the liturgical assembly.

Now, I don't want to appear to be too hard on the academy. Academic theology has an important place in working through aspects of systematic thought that cannot be well explored in a liturgical context—and as I will say below, attempts to insert too much explanatory teaching into a worship context do little to benefit either the learner or the worshiper. The academy itself can also suffer its own peculiar woes, some of them not foreign to a parish, though more often played out in vestry meetings than in the liturgy: arguments about rank and tenure, salary, and schedule. And on the theological side, academics—like all theorists (taking *theory* in its original sense as a worldview, a way of seeing that makes sense of all the evidence)—can become so enamored of their way of seeing that it prevents them seeing things they haven't noticed, or explain them away because they do not quite fit their confirmation bias. In a theological context, ideas about God become so doctrinally fixed and axiomatic that the proponents come to forget they are all approximations, as they must be when talking about God.

Liturgy, of course, can become similarly fossilized if it is not entered into with a like spirit of trepidation concerning shoes on holy ground, and knowledge that the mystery is not to be captured in a syllabus, but experienced in a sacrament. One might think that the obvious connection, both historical and pastoral, between liturgy and faith would need neither defense nor articulation. But Kavanagh confessed to feeling like a voice in the wilderness when recalling theology to its liturgical roots, and cited the fact that academic theologians regard liturgical study as a "less than disciplined swamp in which Anglican high churchmen, Orthodox bishops, and many if not all Roman Catholics and others are hopelessly mired" (46). Liturgy can come to be seen "as a way to evade doctrine" and as no substitute for rigorous study of creeds and confessions (Kevern 12).

While some fuzzy and even erroneous theology can emerge and has emerged from a careless or casual study of liturgy, the church has also produced some equally erring academic theology, and this often happened in those traditions that strayed furthest from the historic shape of the liturgy, caught in a tangle of texts and exhortations and confessions—all of them "about" God, some of them even "preaching Christ," but few of them *making present* the divine reality with the reticent eloquence of water, oil, bread, and wine. As the Puritan divine Richard Baxter noted of his own tradition, "Professors run from sermon to sermon and are never weary of hearing or reading and yet have such languished and starved souls; I know no truer or greater cause than their ignorance and unconscionable neglect of contemplation" (311).

TRIUMPH OF THE JAWBONE

The Reformation might be seen as the triumph of word-*over*-sacrament. Sometimes this is visible in the fabric of a church: all stained glass smashed out, all paintings removed, statues of saints excised or pummeled beyond recognition or adoration—and the only visual relief supplied by a gold-leafed tablet with the text of the Ten Commandments. So earnest were some of the Puritans to wipe out any and all nonverbal symbols that they even objected to a window in Nicholas Ferrar's humble home because the leading between four panes of glass might be mistaken for a cross. Even before the dominance of the Puritan movement, the history of English baptismal rites is instructive. Cranmer shows the process at work in his own revision process—in his various evolving versions of baptism types and shadows have their ending as the newer rite develops—outward and visible signs are excluded one by one as the rites are amended, until we are left with nothing *but* the baby and the bathwater. In place of *physical symbols* of seasoning, restoration, inspiration, coronation, investiture, and enlightenment (which Cranmer considered "dark, dumb ceremonies" but were in their own way eloquent in concrete salt, beeswax, and oil), there is *talk, talk, talk,* admittedly in "a language understood of the people," but translated into English from a deeper and more universal tongue than Latin—the silent language of symbols—into what Hamlet described as "words, words, words." As Paul Tillich noted, the Reformation churches so lost interest in sacramental signs that "even the two remaining sacraments . . . lost their significance, with the result that only the word . . . retained a genuinely sacramental character" (Tillich 94).

Marshall McLuhan famously observed that "the medium is the message"—and in the Reformation move to word over symbol, the medium of the press played a pivotal role. The invention and increased use of the printing press was not so much cause as catalyst in making this shift. Texts, especially printed texts, are portable, atemporal, and after-the-fact; liturgy, on the contrary, can't be packaged and lives in time and space—sanctifying both. Liturgy at its best is like any great event—"You just had to *be* there."

Text seems to have won the day. In spite of the fruits of the liturgical revival and the generally high place liturgy holds in the modern church, the Reformation has largely had its way even in those parts of the church that most fervently resisted it. Roman Catholics and Episcopalians alike have focused much of their liturgical renewal and revision on texts that change their *thou*s to *you*s, or texts that include or expand to vary how God is portrayed in what is called "verbal imagery"—a peculiar usage that indicates how accustomed we have become to think of words instead of icons as images. And while many of the texts of modern liturgies are *shorter*, for some reason they seem *wordier* and less eloquent than their forebears.

This is not meant to suggest that the text of liturgies is unimportant; there is power in the boldly preached text, the clearly proclaimed gospel, and the inspiration of poetic language. But the words of liturgy should form an integrated whole with the ritual action, not serve as cover or, as is too often the case, play-by-play description of—or even substitution for—ritual action. For example, some parishes with splendid liturgies will so arrange their worship that as soon as any ritual action for which words are *not* provided happens, the people are sent to a hymnal or missalette or bulletin so that the procession or the censing or whatever wordless ritual act is taking place is effectively unseen and unwitnessed by those who are singing words, able to glimpse the action at most between verses or from the corner of an eye. Are we too shy simply to stand and watch the drama as *living* images of God, our sisters and brothers, bring forward the gifts, prepare the table, and bid us come to the supper of the

Lamb? We would rather miss the irony, and sing "Let all mortal flesh keep silence," than take our own advice, shut our mouths, raise our eyes, and contemplate the awesome mystery unfolding among us and with us and through us and set before us.

For we participate far more fully in the action by observation than by parallel verbal exercises not unlike the "people's mass books" or other pious devotions of the pre- and Counter-Reformation. One of my favorite icons, a large instance of which stood at the entry to the nave of the Cathedral of Saint John the Divine, and of which I was inspired to sketch a contemporary version, is entitled, "Saint John in Silence." To ensure his silence John deliberately presses a finger against his lips to keep them closed. The one who witnessed the liturgy of heaven from Patmos knows the wisdom of being simply speechless.

A contemporary take on the image of John in Silence

And so, sometimes, should we be: there are times, after all, when, tempted as we are to fill the silence with our chatter, it is best to be instructed, "Don't just do something; *stand* there!"

If this indictment is true, that liturgy has become part of the information age rather than corporeal engagement with the mystery beyond comprehension, if the jawbone has triumphed even in the *liturgical* churches, what will they do when the wood is dry? In short, is there any hope for a second wave of liturgical renewal, one not focused primarily on the text and secondary theological deconstruction, but on recovery of the treasures of sight and sound that have been cast down or cast aside, or that have grown old and are in need of restoration? I am tempted to join Edmund Sears in saying, "O hush your noise, ye men of strife, and hear the angels sing!"

I began my adult work life in the theater, so I can't resist an illustration from that craft, which began its life in Greece as liturgy, and reemerged in the early church in the same way, to become "show business" in the West only when the churches finally expelled the performers. A young playwright approached the inimitable impresario David Belasco, telling him, "Mr. Belasco, I have a wonderful idea for a play." Belasco responded curtly, "Send it to me on a postcard." Whereupon the young man, deeply offended, replied, "Oh, Mr. Belasco, I couldn't possibly fit my idea on a postcard." To which the producer responded, "Then you haven't got an idea."

In the present context, if you can't express it in liturgy, then you haven't got a theology. We can, after all, fool ourselves that all our words have somehow tamed the mystery; we comfort ourselves with language by giving tidy names to incurable diseases. We can come to think that because we can recite the Athanasian or the Nicene Creed that somehow the Trinity is a little less off-putting—but are those creeds, or the reams of theological bickering and analogizing about the Trinity, really any more eloquent than Rublev's angelic icon of the hospitality of Abraham? If God deigns to be at home with us, we had best let God do the talking, as our mortal flesh keeps silence and serves.

Things may be changing, of course. There is hope for a recovered role for liturgy as a predominant vehicle for the church's self-expression.

A new generation has arrived for whom the visual is once again a primary means of communication, though the icons appear in glowing diodes on a monitor instead of tempera on a board. The modern media have rediscovered the synergy of word and image, and people are coming to expect this unity of vision and meaning, expressed through clearly spoken word accompanied by eloquent gesture or image.

Polish playwright Stanisław Ignacy Witkiewicz tragically took his own life in 1939 as his world was falling apart between the assaults of the Nazis and the Soviets. Harking back to the roots of the theater as religious ceremony, Witkiewicz felt that it was the theater's task to try to recapture the sense of the mystery of existence that had once been the domain of religion. I, for one, have not given up on the church yet—I did come to the church *from* the theater, after all—and I believe the church to be capable of recovering its old territory, of restoring and reconsecrating the churches that have been turned into dance halls or condominiums and making them the centers of a revitalized and liturgical theology.

This time around, the church will be challenged by a generation handy with tablets other than those given at Sinai, a generation for whom icons are not windows into heaven but just part of the user interface. The mistake we would make as liturgists would be to try to match CGI cinema in delivering a dazzling display. What the new generation will be seeking in the church is not further sensory overload, but the clean and meaningful, artfully simple, transparent lo-tech miracles of faith boldly proclaimed, of candles, crosses, banners, upraised hands and voices, the powerful unison of Gregorian chant, a spark struck at the end of a fast, a sudden splash of water, a loaf of bread broken, and a cup of wine shared.

These powerful symbolic actions and sounds arise from a deep tradition in the church, but also from even deeper parts of the human psyche, a collective unconscious or shadowed subconscious harking back to preliterate and perhaps even prelingual times. Reviving their use may to some extent make up for the loss of a truly common language of faith at the linguistic level. The fragmentation of previously common liturgies into a cloud of optional forms and the proliferation of modern Bible translations have robbed the church of the allusive and almost incantational quality with which time and tradition imbued the Tudor and Caroline Book of Common Prayer, and the Jacobean version of the Bible; much as the introduction of the vernacular in the modern Roman rite has demystified, but also tamed, the evocative power of a special sacred manner of speech, with the consequential linguistic division of congregations into separate worshiping communities. This is not a call for a return to hocus-pocus, but an acknowledgment that there is a character to the language of worship that distinguishes it from casual conversation, just as there are special times, places, and actions that form and inform the context of worship, set apart from the mundane by the act of *devotion*.

CODA

Clearly, we need words. If we didn't, I'd stop writing right now. But too much trust in words, especially when divorced from the acts to which they relate, or even worse replacing or subsuming those acts, can prove the means of our undoing. Those who in a dark primeval time sought to preserve their unity by building a tower to heaven were undone by the loss of *meaning* through the multiplication of *language*.

A return to the principles of liturgical theology may yet serve to rattle our verbal towers that, like the proud city of Babel, are no less full of knowledge without wisdom, of speech without meaning, of form without substance, of running starving from text to text without the food of contemplation. When we are shaken from complacent secondary spin doctoring and face the awesome and tremendous Holy Mystery in a primeval forest, amidst standing stones, by whitewashed adobe, in a silent hermit's anchorhold, or in a towering nave; when we have gone through the little blue door and carried the weighty cross down a long and smoke-filled aisle while rows of devout believers bow in reverence to the symbol of the unspoken and unspeakable Word above all words and worlds—then, and only then, as Canon West said, will it be time to talk about our religion.

Julian of Norwich

Ascetics and Aesthetics

The Trinity Whom We Adore

Of a sudden, the Trinity filled my heart with joy. And so I understood it shall be in heaven without end to all that shall come there. For the Trinity is God, God is the Trinity; the Trinity is our maker and keeper, the Trinity is our everlasting lover, everlasting joy and bliss, through our Lord Jesus Christ. And this was shown to me in the first, and in all of the showings; for where Jesus appears there is the blessed Trinity understood, as I see it. (Julian 4)

✦ ✦ ✦

Our vicar is like God: invisible on weekdays and incomprehensible on Sundays. —words attributed to an English parish warden

Speaking of words, more of them have been spoken, more ink has been spilled, and probably more blood shed and more confusion generated on account of the Holy Trinity than any other Christian doctrine. I alluded to the spillage of ink, multiplied by the printing press, in the previous chapter, where I favored the ritual over the pedantic. So in this chapter I want to begin by following through, and I hope delivering on something of what I promised, in thinking about the Trinity not so much doctrinally as liturgically. My principal reason for this lies in the absolute uniqueness of God. Anything one says about God will fall short. All analogies ultimately fail because nothing is perfectly analogous to God.

Classical theology says that God's uniqueness lies in God's essence being the same as God's existence. To put it another way, only God possesses God-ness, and God-ness is the only quality God has; God-ness is what God *is*; or even more bluntly, echoing the *Shema*, only God is God and God is only God. All of the attributes of God—power, wisdom, love—relate to the activities of God in creation and redemption and sanctification. They describe What God Has Done, but not Who God Is. When God allowed Moses to glimpse the Presence on Mount Sinai, God only permitted him to see God's back after having passed him by (Exod. 33:18–23); in one sense all that we see of God is the wake of God's passage, the wonders of creation and salvation, culminating in the great work accomplished on the cross, from which Christ declares, "It is finished." That clearest self-manifestation of God reveals God's *love* (the greatest love that gives up the self for the other). It was in the contemplation of that love that Dame Julian of Norwich experienced the closest one can come to the apprehension of God's God-ness. It was a revelation of the love of God that led her into deep and confounding contemplation of Mystery.

And when we come to the Trinity, we are even more apt to be confounded. This is especially true when an effort is made to unpack or explicate the doctrine rather than to contemplate the Mystery. It is perilously easy to forget that all of our analogies and definitions are approximations, and that we dare not transform our building blocks into foundation stones—rejecting and replacing the One we have been given. So how to proceed?

First of all, I would start with the assertion that the Trinity is not a doctrine, but a Person—in fact, three Persons. "Trinity" is the name by which theologians have chosen to identify the God whom we worship, the God we know—insofar as we can know God—as Father, and Son, and Holy Spirit: and we get that triune title from the liturgy of baptism, with which it is linked by Christ himself in the charge issued in the penultimate verse of Matthew's Gospel (28:19), where the disciples are told to *do* it, not to talk about it. The point is, of course, that we worship even while we do not fully know as we are known. Like the Athenians of Acts 17:23, all of us to some extent worship an unknown God, or at least a God not fully known—yet faith and grace drive and support our worship even by means of the partial knowledge that we have. God has not left us entirely clueless, as Paul told the Athenians. And as Julian herself reminds us, God gave three gifts, an ABC as it were, to further us along, so that here on earth, reviewing the wake of God's passing, we can have a little of the knowledge that we will have in full measure in heaven. The three gifts Julian discerned are natural reason, the teaching of the church, and the gift of the Holy Spirit (80). We are far from comfortless, far from totally clueless.

Among the data which we gather from this threefold gift of partial knowledge, the fruit of the baptismal ordinance, is the firm belief that God is One in Three, a Trinity in Unity, a love so powerful and cosmic that it had to be dynamic—and paradoxical. And so we give our God the name of Trinity, for this is the only way we have to grasp even the hem of the transcendent garment. Though there are many doctrines *about* the Trinity, many unpackings of the meaning of this name, the Trinity God's-self is not a doctrine to be discussed but a *mystery to be contemplated and adored*.

Now, in theology—especially liturgical theology—unlike in detective stories, a mystery isn't a puzzle we can figure out if only we are given enough clues. In liturgical theology, we are reminded that the *mystery* is the old Greek word for *sacrament*—not something to be solved through an exercise of the little gray cells, but rather something to be experienced as an exercise—an *askesis*—of the *whole* self, with, above all, as George Herbert said, the heart bearing the longest part, as the whole world in every corner sings, "my God and King."

A mystery, a sacrament, is something a bit like the Doctor's blue box, the TARDIS (Time and Relative Dimension in Space) that brings us beyond surface appearances to some deeper or higher thing—so effectively that it becomes a means to experience that deeper or higher reality. There is always more than meets the eye in a sacrament: there is always some inward reality to which the outward, visible appearance directs, draws, invites, and brings us. The water of baptism and the bread and wine of the Eucharist embody truths that verbal doctrine cannot express, truths not simply assented to with the mind, but experienced with the whole self—living truths from the hand of the one who *is* living, loving Truth.

This doesn't mean that theologians have given up trying to understand or communicate these truths in other ways, though the effort is much like translating poetry into prose. Often, rather than deepening our understanding only confusion results. Worse than that, over the years theologians' efforts to define exactly how (and if) baptism renews or regenerates, or how bread and wine can (or can't) be at the same time the body and blood of Christ, have led to division and persecution in the church. The church has often forgotten the wisdom that C.S. Lewis encapsulated in his brief epigram, that Christ's commandment was, "'Take, eat'; not 'Take, understand'" (*Letters to Malcolm*, 104).

The same is true of efforts to "explain" or "understand" the Trinity—and I am not about to add to the succession of failed attempts. Rather, I invite us to approach the Trinity much as we do the eucharistic bread and wine, as a sacrament to contemplate and experience rather than as a proposition to analyze. Just as the bread and wine of the Eucharist are not about baking and wine-making (though these arts have a place in bringing the sacrament to fulfillment), so too the Trinity is not about precise definitions of craftily constructed Greek and Latin formulas meant to rule the limits beyond which speculation might be carried forward, and outside of whose bounds we stray into the dangerous territory of heresy. Our efforts at understanding, our doctrinal formulations and creeds, for all their usefulness in defining boundaries, are at best thumbnail sketches of the Being and Loving and Doing who lies behind and beyond all that is. In one sense, the best thing to say about the Trinity is the Nicene Creed, and leave it at that.

I mentioned *askesis* in passing a few moments ago, and I want to expand a bit on its implications. The popular mind links asceticism with *not* doing things—but the word means *exercise* or *practice*, or as we might say, *discipline*. The point of ascetical poverty, for instance, is not impoverishment, the absence of possessions, but freedom from attachment *to* them, the ability to subsist without entanglement, or as Saint Gregory the Great once said, to make use of the things of this world without being ensnared by them. I recall a conversation with a monk who returned his membership pin (in an organization of which we both were members) with a kind note saying that his community didn't pin anything on their habits. This has remained a wonderful image for me: ascetics are people who don't have things clipped to them, people who aren't "pinned" down, unlabeled people who are truly free because they have given themselves away to the One-in-Three, the source of all life and freedom. In a way, the one living the ascetical life is the one who knows *things* best, for she will have them in perspective, at arm's length, far enough away to be seen, reflected upon, and made proper use of as needed, without worrying whether there will be enough, who has more or better, where the next one is coming from—because it is all a gift. At the same time, the ascetic will be one close to God, thoroughly known by God, able to participate in the divine life that does not consist in the abundance of possessions, but in the transparency of personhood.

As I said, the world sees asceticism primarily in terms of lack and austerity. And it is true that some ascetical enthusiasts have afflicted themselves with penances and hardships. Thank goodness for Julian's sane and gentle rebuttal to that tendency, that "it is not God's will that we follow the feelings of pain, in sorrow and mourning because of them, but at once pass beyond them and hold ourselves in endless delight" (15). Harsh, austere, and self-wounding asceticism turns our attention toward ourselves and our pains, while the contemplation of *Christ's* passion and our participation in it turns us toward God "in endless delight."

True asceticism is a kind of disciplined awareness of relationships freed from the desire to possess and control, awareness of relationships between the self and the other, that other who is God or neighbor, or God *in* neighbor. And this awareness, cultivated through the disciplined exercise of the Christian life, may explain the paradoxical spiritual richness that monks and nuns experience in spite of the sometimes external austerity of their lives; they enjoy the rich harvest of contemplation—which is, in some ways, the simplest liturgical act we undertake when we remove our worldly shoes and kneel on holy ground before a flame that burns but does not consume. In these moments the soul is stilled and receptive before the One-in-Three who simply Is.

Contemplation is the practice and discipline of engaged disengagement. It is not to be mistaken for passivity, as if the contemplative were simply part of an audience looking on with the view to amusement or diversion. On the contrary, *diversion* is just what contemplation isn't. Just as the world mistakes poverty for impoverishment, it looks at contemplation and sees stasis, or self-absorption. But the contemplative is inwardly active at the level of the soul, participating intimately, not static but *ec*statically absorbed completely with the divine other, and *ascetic*—exercising inwardly, fanning the warmth of the divine spark within, dancing with God, totally God-absorbed, experiencing God's revelation not only in ruminating over words uttered in the distant past, records of the traces of God's wake, but in hearing new promises spoken in their personal present, or read by that glowing flame that burns but does not consume, savoring the words written long ago on stone and parchment, and exulting in the wordless words inscribed on their human hearts.

Thus absorbed in the Holy Trinity, we come to know God; but we also come to know ourselves. As Julian said:

> God is nearer to us than our own soul. . . . for our soul sits at rest in God, and our soul stands in strength in God, and our soul is rooted in God in endless love. And therefore if we wish to know our soul . . . we must seek our lord God *in whom it is enclosed*. (56)

We join this ascetical and liturgical theological exercise, this divine dance, by virtue of our membership and participation in a church that prays for all who seek God, or a deeper knowledge of God. And so the Trinity stands before us, and we stand *in* the Trinity, not as a doctrine but as a mysterious revelation of the heart of God—reminding us of the vital role of contemplation in the growth and nurture of the Christian soul.

Contemplation can take many liturgical forms: centering prayer (including the Jesus Prayer), in which a short phrase or word is repeated in conjunction with the easy flow of one's own breath, distractions gently allowed to flow past, as the pray-er and prayer settle into each other; *lectio divina*, in which scriptural (or devotional) texts are mindfully savored in small sips to extract every last nuance of spiritual flavor; or contemplation of a visual image—a natural scene, a candle flame, or an icon. Whatever form of contemplation is employed, it remains crucial to understand it as a means, not as an end.

This ascetical approach, the spiritual discipline of prayer and presence, is focused but not obsessive: as I noted earlier, monastics have perspective because they exercise what the Dominican Meister Eckhart called *abgescheidenheit*—detachment or "letting-go-ness." Or to use the image I mentioned earlier, they are not pinned or clipped to things. And this balanced engagement is important for us as liturgical theologians.

Look at what happens when liturgical things *are* "attached" or pinned down instead: in Corinth, for example, where things went terribly wrong. Paul warned that congregation, so caught up in its internal disagreements that it had forgotten the reason for its weekly gathering: to worship, honor, and seek to know the God who called its members into fellowship. His warning holds for us today, for we too live in the "already but not yet" that lies between creation and culmination; the urge to want to pin things down in a time of uncertainty and liminality is great; labels are so tempting and categories so seductive; and as events of recent years have shown, the church today is just as much caught up in the tendency to shadowbox with its own inadequacies as was the church of Corinth.

Whenever the church gets so caught up in seeking to define or limit the means of grace that it forgets about the hope of glory, and thereby obstructs or withholds this grace-giving power, the church is in trouble. What can be more absurd than arguing about worship? From what we can tell about the church in Corinth—based on Paul's letters and correspondence from Clement a generation later—this was a congregation that never quite "got it." And what they didn't "get" was that the sacraments and the gifts of the Spirit are meant to point beyond themselves to God. Sacraments are means, not ends. People are ends, not means. And the Corinthians had it backwards. By the close of his association with them,

Paul was clearly exasperated, suggesting tearing the whole thing down and starting over. They had turned the Eucharist into a dinner party, and had come to see speaking in tongues as an end in itself. They got caught up in the personalities of the apostles instead of heeding their teaching and direction. They were, strictly speaking, shallow: caught up in the surface—attached and clipped and pinned to it, if you will—and could not see beyond what meets the eye, all the while considering themselves especially profound and holy. They were so worried about idolatry that their very worry became a kind of idol in itself. They missed the truth that the primary difference between an idol and a sacrament is that the sacrament is a means to bring us to something greater, while the idol is an end in itself. Those who worship idols, however holy they appear, are clipped to the level of what meets the eye, like water beetles skimming busily on the surface and all the while dying of thirst. What is needed—and what spiritual disciplines of prayer and meditation offer the church—is the true gift of contemplation, which can look past the reflective surfaces by calmly ignoring the flickering lights, so that the one who contemplates can see the everlasting rocky foundation of the stream below.

In the end, contemplation is the liturgy of heaven. Because there is always more to God than meets the eye, even the eye of faith, we will never be bored with God. The Trinity has been doing that inward dynamic dance of God's own self-subsisting uncreated existence, God simply being who God is in uncontainable joy and love, from before time and forever. And we are invited, plucked from our wallflower seats to join that dance, to contemplate and participate in that divine energy, that love that drives the sun and the other stars. That is what we do wherever, together, we gather. My invitation to you is to take every opportunity to look at the record of God's saving deeds, and at humanity's struggling, stumbling, and sometimes surprisingly graceful efforts to respond. By beginning with the Trinity, we trust that by contemplation on the saving story of what *God has done*, we can discern the traces of the untellable reality of *who God is*.

We've seen, from the example of Corinth, how *not* to proceed—but even in their failure there is guidance for a better way. I said before that the Corinthians were clipped and pinned to surface issues, converting means to ends. The problem in part was that they were looking at the wrong surfaces. They were looking at dividing walls when they should have been looking into each other's faces.

And we know the reason for this. However much the natural world can tell us about who God is, however much is revealed about God in the mighty acts of grace and salvation, however much is captured in the words of theologians and the liturgies of worshipers, the most powerful and revealing thing God has ever done was to create creatures bearing an echo of the divine image and likeness; and then, in the fullness of time, to become incarnate in that same image of *who God is*. If we want to know what God is like, we can find no better start than by looking at each other, at our brothers and sisters, each of whom is a living, breathing sacrament of God. And in them and through them we will *find* God, and in God we will find ourselves, all enclosed, as Julian said, wrapped in the threefold love of God the Three-in-One.

I will take up this theme at greater length in reflecting on the art and use of icons, but for now I simply note, in relation to the life of monastics and married both, those whose chastity is bound by a vow of celibacy or a vow of fidelity, that this is where their *askesis*, their discipline, comes in: for the chaste soul, whether single or wed, treats the other with the respect due a child of God, never as a means, but always as an end. What we are forbidden to do with objects and liturgies—treating them as ends in themselves—we are charged to do with people. This is why Paul concludes his poignant appeal to the Corinthians by urging them to agree with each other, to be at peace, and to kiss each other. When we have quieted our family struggles in the church, calmed the reflecting surface so that recognizable likenesses emerge, we can then take the next step, beyond the mirror's surface, to look to Christ, the pioneer and perfecter of our faith, who is himself the perfect revelation of God.

Coming to agreement and peace in the church will mean further detachment, giving in and giving up—to use worship's phrase: it will mean the sacrifice and oblation of ourselves. Each of us will have to step off our own little pedestal if we are to reach each other and face each other and embrace each other in the holy kiss of peace. Each of us will have to take off those worldly shoes to tread on holy ground.

In this very action the echo of our divine likeness is revealed, and the sacramental nature of this mystery blossoms and bears fruit, enabled by the gift of the Holy Spirit. This is what Jesus did in becoming one of us. This is what Julian experienced when she chose to find no heaven other than that which is revealed in Jesus Christ, and him in his passion (19). This is what God did in risking the creation of creatures that would be capable of being truly free—which means creatures capable of rejecting their Creator. In the paschal giving of ourselves to help another, in setting aside our own needs for the sake of one whose need is greater, our resemblance to God emerges, and we become recognizable as what we are meant to be, as our own passing wake of loving action limns the outline of who we are: the children of God.

In doing this we go beyond what meets the eye, into what meets the mind, heart, and spirit, like speaking to like in the wordless communion of God with God's creation. In embracing our brothers and sisters, we are reenacting and celebrating and contemplating the cosmic turnabout when Love Divine came down and lived among us as one of us, and we penetrate beneath the surface and see beyond what meets the eye to what enlivens the mind, touches the heart, and lifts the spirit. We encounter and contemplate the Trinity: *who God is* in all richness and infinite variety. As Julian portrays God speaking:

> That I am: the might and the goodness of fatherhood. That I am: the wisdom of motherhood. That I am: the light and the grace that is all blessed love. That I am: the Trinity. That I am: the Unity. I am the sovereign goodness of all manner of things. I am that which makes you love. I am that which makes you long. That I am: the endless fulfillment of all true desires. (59)

For the Trinity is the Giver, the Gift, and the Giving—the one great God, so in love with the world that creation itself will not be complete until the Triune Name of Father, Son, and Holy Spirit is carried to the ends of the world, and everything that has breath praises the Lord in the never-ending dance of contemplation whose center and whose music is the Trinity.

3

The Lost Coin

Human Roles and Divine Images

The church's liturgy, in word and action, is in intimate relationship with the church's theology: the liturgy expresses the theological mind of the church, but it also informs and forms it, from the individual parish to each whole tradition—Roman Catholic, Anglican, Lutheran, or Orthodox. One aspect of this theology—the set of doctrines and attitudes of any given body of believers—concerns how those believers see and understand sex and sexuality, both in human lives and as attributed to the divine life by analogy. These beliefs will also shape and be shaped by worship, in practical ways, including how they speak of people, and how they speak of God and imagine God (that is, how they *picture* the invisible), and how churches will understand and impose limits on the ministries and rites available to, and performed by, the church's ministers and members, influenced by these choices in language and image.

It is no secret that the Christian tradition has a long history of sexism—a preference for *the male*, sometimes rising to the level of exclusivity, embodied in the predominant use of male language and imagery for God and (in some churches) the restriction of ordained (and sometimes, lay) ministry to men. These often go together, and reflect the cultures in which Christianity emerged and developed. In those contexts words with *masculine* gender expressed universal referents, and one could say, "Man is a mammal with large external breasts" without irony. The purpose of this chapter is to examine how this tradition has been maintained and reinforced—and resisted and reformed—by aspects of the liturgical practices of the church, beginning with the quest to use *inclusive* language for people, and *expansive* language for God.

Before proceeding, however, it is important to acknowledge that *inclusive* or *gender-neutral* language for people has become standard in much of the worldly world. This is a double-edged sword: the church that continues to use traditional Tudor English for its worship may be one of the few places where people will encounter such archaic forms of language—apart from performances of Shakespeare. That will be off-putting to some, but it will form an attraction for others who want their worship to be *different* from their day-to-day experience. Any changes in language and ritual ought to be approached with care and consideration of what is gained and what may be lost in the process.

However, the goal of this essay is to explore the ways in which adaptations in our worship forms can be grounded in the recovery of the "lost coin"—neglected or devalued strands of the tradition—and how the deep roots of tradition might play a role in renovation and renewal.

Missing Persons

The liturgical devaluation of women can be simple or complex; it may occur in isolated instances or as a systematic program, as a long-continued habit of neglect or as a deliberate choice to obscure. It may rest (as indeed it did for many centuries of the church's life, based in large part on the role of Eve in Genesis) on a defective anthropology that sees women as functionally inferior to men—weak, irrational, easily swayed, incapable or unskilled. It may also arise from a desire to universalize some of the qualities of certain women to the sex as a whole, and limit functions on the basis of an alleged natural gift for *nurture* as opposed to one for *leadership*. It may pick up a metaphor from the Pauline tradition (that the husband is the head of the wife) while ignoring another (that in Christ there is no more male and female, but all are one). The selective pressure of these traditions, and their embodiment in the liturgy and polity of the churches, have tended to keep women out of positions of responsibility and leadership in most of the Christian world. This was true in the Episcopal Church until very recently. We tend to forget that women were first licensed as lay readers as recently as 1969, and as deputies to the General Convention only in 1970; ordination to the priesthood and episcopate came a few years later. All of this is still well within living memory.

So how do we work liturgically to amend this pervasive pressure against seeing women in an equal light? One minor corrective for which I have long campaigned—and which some may see as trivial—is elevating the observance of the celebration of Mary and Martha of Bethany from its current status as a commemoration to that of major feast. These saints—about whom scripture attests far more than it does for all but a handful of the twelve apostles—have for too long been relegated to second-class status in the calendar, and it is high time that these women, held up for centuries as archetypes of the contemplative and active lives of prayer, be given due honor along with Mary Magdalene and the other leading apostles and disciples.

Given the principle embodied in the phrase *lex orandi lex credendi*—the law of prayer and the law of belief in dialogue—faith experience, if not faith itself, shapes and is shaped by liturgical experience. This includes the liturgical experience of the Bible itself, how the Bible is used in worship, which for many today is their sole exposure to the sacred text. The days when the home was a normative place for Bible study are long past. Television's electronic hearth replaced the family gathering to study God's word, and has itself been replaced more and more by essentially private tablets and mobile phones—on which I dare say the biblical texts rarely appear. Few people keep a Bible by their bedside for private devotional reading, and those Gideon Bibles in hotel rooms likely remain untouched by anything but socks and hankies. Sunday school and programs for the young, along with adult Bible study, continue, of course, but with the general decline in the power of Christendom, even these contexts have ceased to engage more than a fraction of the general—and even Christian—culture.

Historically, this kind of intensive and intentional Bible study only existed for a brief time to any wide popular extent—beginning only with the advent of printing and vernacular translations in readily available editions. Given that the wider church has not always been keen on individuals studying the scriptures without pastoral guidance, the idea of private (or corporate but nonliturgical) Bible study only really came to the fore in the Reformation, with the vision of every boy at the plow and weaver at the loom knowing more scripture than a bishop. Before and since, the main place the scripture was and is heard and expounded is within the context of the liturgy. This means that characters and images excluded from the liturgical lectionary are effectively invisible, such as Rachel's children, as if they were not important.

In the mid-1980s, Marjorie Procter-Smith undertook a study of the Common Lectionary (used, with adaptation and some variation, in the majority of liturgical churches then using a set lectionary). She found that out of a total of 545 biblical passages, spread out over the 3 years of the lectionary cycle, only 110 readings concerned women (in either a good or bad light) or used a feminine image for God. Of these, in only 36 were the women or the images significant or principal: only 6.6 percent of the widely used set of scripture readings portrayed a major female character, personality, or image.

The current Revised Common Lectionary was designed in part to rectify this situation. A few examples of improvements include: John 20:11–18, recording Mary Magdalene's encounter with the risen Christ, is no longer optional for Easter in Year A; and the testimony of the Samaritan woman to her townspeople (John 4:28–30) is no longer optional on the Third Sunday in Lent in the same year; nor is the passage describing Jesus's relationship with Mary, Martha, and Lazarus (John 11:1–16) two weeks later on the Fifth Sunday in Lent. Several important women are now included in the Sunday cycle: the long-suffering woman who dared to touch the hem of Jesus's garment (Mark 5:25–34), and the woman freed from her arthritic infirmity (Luke 13:10–17). The question that must be asked is, Why were they not included for so long?

Still missing in action are Matthew's version (26:6–13) of the woman anointing Jesus prior to his passion, though her synoptic twin (Mark

14:3–9) does make an appearance on Palm Sunday in Year B—if, that is, those who plan the liturgy include Mark 14 in the already long liturgy of the day. It is a supreme irony that this optional passage includes the verse, "Truly I tell you, wherever the good news is proclaimed in the whole world, what she has done will be told in remembrance of her" (14:9)—except where the rector wants to save a few minutes in the liturgy.

That being said, the Revised Common Lectionary marked a huge step toward providing congregations with liturgical exposure to passages of scripture that most will never have encountered previously. Parishes that make use of the first of the two alternative "tracks" of readings from the Hebrew Scriptures on the Sundays after Pentecost will also hear passages in which women play leading roles, such as those represented by Ruth and Naomi, or roles of actual leadership, such as that of Deborah. Again, however, this part of the cycle is optional, and many parishes will continue to use either the BCP Lectionary, or track two of the Revised Common Lectionary which is based on the typological principle that informed the earlier BCP version: the lesson from the Hebrew Scriptures is chosen to complement a theme or aspect of the Gospel appointed for the day. Many preachers prefer this thematic approach, while others will enjoy the opportunity to explore more of the sacred story laid out in track one, especially if there is interest in exposing a congregation to a wider selection of scripture. (Whether the liturgy is the best place for such exposure is another question: when my Bronx parish used track one, the adult Bible study was geared to support and connect the nominally "continuous" cycle of readings of the Hebrew Scriptures and fill any gaps in what is of necessity a bare selection of passages.)

Until the advent of the Revised Common Lectionary, the bulk of the Episcopal Church's lay leadership, and not a small portion of its clergy—apart from those engaged in intensive Bible study or the recital of the Daily Office with its own much more inclusive lectionary—had been formed and informed by a small, selective digest of scripture, one that omitted much of the witness to the role and place of women in the story of salvation. Many Episcopalians have at last begun to be exposed to some of these women and their stories.

Their Roman Catholic cousins, on the other hand (in the current approved lectionary), will still be missing most of these witnesses and their testimony. Ruth and Naomi are absent; Deborah's rule of Israel is unacknowledged; the long-suffering woman who dared touch the hem of Jesus's garment and the arthritic woman bound and bent in pain are both still waiting for a cure; and, if the parish chooses the shorter version of the Passion for Palm Sunday B, the woman whose story was to be remembered wherever the Gospel is heard will not be called to mind. Such gaps cannot but have impact on how people understand the work of salvation, and the roles that women have played in it. The examples of faith, leadership, and courage will not be there for admiration or emulation.

One might well argue that what is (or was) missing in the cycle of readings is more than compensated for in the cycle of commemorations of saints—and surely it is true that the calendars of all of the liturgical churches are full of exemplary people, many of them women. However, exposure to such ideal (if not idolized) female figures may not have impact on how much women are encouraged or allowed to do, or what ministries they can perform in those churches. Perhaps the starkest contrast is in the gap between the exaltation of Mary the Theotokos, the Blessed Virgin, and the strict limits on the ministry of women in the churches where the Mother of God is most venerated; even revival of the diaconate, attested in scripture as an office held by women in the apostolic era, is still only on the verge of consideration or guarded acceptance in much of the church catholic. So any possible elevation to red-letter status for Mary and Martha of Bethany on the Episcopal calendar, which I mentioned at the beginning of this chapter, may have less impact than desired, if it were merely as a token of respect rather than as a call to emulation.

Neglected Images: Lost and Found

The language of liturgy expresses belief—sometimes definitively so in the recitation of the Nicene and Apostles' Creeds, though, as noted elsewhere in this volume, the mere recitation of a text does not always indicate full understanding of, or full agreement with, the words being recited. The recitation can become *pro forma* and the content relegated to an aspiration rather than a firm belief. Fingers may not be crossed, but the mind may well wander.

Still, language retains its power. One aspect of language that has come under revision in the last half-century or so concerns the ways in which sex and gender are portrayed. Previously widely accepted forms of English speech, such as the generic use of masculine nouns and pronouns to represent both men and women, have become far less acceptable to many, and perhaps most, modern ears. New translations of the Bible used in worship have sought to address this concern, as have revisions of liturgical texts, both rites and hymns. While usually successful and sometimes graceful, in the effort to render texts inclusive while preserving their doctrine or sentiment, the translations and revisions have sometimes failed to maintain aspects of their underlying original texts or versions. Slight shifts in language, undertaken for the sound reason of making texts more inclusive, can have unintended consequences of changed meaning and altered emotional impact. That being said, although there is some continued discomfort around inclusive language for human beings (such as doubts about the propriety of using *they* in the singular), the level of discomfort increases considerably when we come to *expansive* language to describe God.

Some of those most opposed to such language have occasionally expressed themselves in ways which a cooler temper and more reflection might have restrained. For example, some have claimed that such language changes our "understanding of God" or even "the nature of God." The first is presumptuous—no one can reasonably claim to understand God, and there are many different and equally valid limited *understandings*. The second betrays a kind of platonic attitude toward language, which treats words as having, rather than conveying, meaning. It also imbues language with a kind of magic power, as if our describing a wall as blue made it blue, or anything we could say about God might possibly change God—rather than changing our own thoughts about God.

Of course, those who say these latter things (I hope) do not mean them literally. They mean something like, "If we change language about God, people will come to have ideas about God that don't fit the revealed knowledge we have." And so far, so true. The problem is that they may have allowed the language they use to slip in just such a wrong direction, toward the literal, away from the analogical. The question is, How useful is the revealed knowledge of God, and is such revelation—given the fact that God has depths we can never plumb—at an end? And have we ever gotten it wrong?

The situation becomes most difficult when someone takes a poetic image and applies it as if it were a datum within our control. Truly, God *is* our Father, but not in the same sense that the will is the father of the deed, or that William was my father, or that George Washington was "father of his country." Language about God is not God, but it can form how we think of God, how we relate to God, and this is true even of the language of revelation committed to us in scripture.

A dip into Aquinas might be helpful here. He held that language about God had to be analogically predicated. Anything you *predicate* (that is, declare or affirm) about God has to be in the form of analogy. The other forms of predication are *univocal* and *equivocal*. The first assumes that the quality you declare is the same in all places you declare it: a red shoe and a red hat (and let's be technical and say of the same wavelength of light) share the same *redness*. The second assumes that the quality or term you declare is different in its different instances: for example, a Labrador is a breed of dog, but also a region of Canada—note that the two uses of the same name are related, but the dog *is not* the province and *is* of a wholly different sort of being. Aquinas holds that neither of these modes quite work when talking about God, largely because of God's absolute simplicity and uniqueness: as I noted in the previous chapter, only God has God-ness and God-ness is all that God has; God-ness is what God *is*. So Aquinas reminds us to sit easily with our God-talk, and realize that any attribute we declare about God is by way of analogy: we can talk about God being great or good with great or good created things in our minds, but only as pointers to the otherwise indescribable character of God.

The problem with such language arises when people start to slip out of analogical predication, particularly in a univocal direction, thinking that God is Father in the same way a man is a father. When *Father* is applied analogically to God, it does not mean that God is male, or that God is the source of my Y-chromosome. But that is just where the slippage begins to happen. God can be predicated to have the *character* of a father (loving, caring, creative, protective) without also attributing to God the *characteristics* of a man (trivial ones, such as having a beard, or more important ones, like being male).

But first things first: let's agree from the outset that God is not male—or female, or both. Maleness itself is not some Platonic form that exists in eternity as the opposite to femaleness in a dualistic dance of yin and yang; and even if you are a Platonist and think these forms exist independently of their expression in concrete things, they are still not God. God is beyond all such categories and consequences of limitation, the various qualities we use to distinguish one thing from another. God is not a thing, not even the very best thing; not just a "supreme being"— not even Anselm's clever but ultimately unsatisfying "that than which nothing is greater"—but Being Itself. As Isaac Asimov once quipped in a talk about the book of Job, "God is God and you aren't." God is incomprehensible, and any terms we use in an effort to comprehend God will be limited, partial, and inadequate. We'll take a further look at God in the next chapter, but here I want to focus on what approximate good any of our language can be to help us understand something *about* God, even if we cannot comprehend God.

We are left with this problem concerning the negative reception the use of expansive language for God has often received: "Why is it that those who have difficulty picturing the First Person of the Trinity as Mother have no difficulty picturing the Second Person as a Lamb and the Third Person as a Dove?" It might be quickly argued that the latter two images are biblical, while the first isn't; and, following the rules of iconography laid down in Eastern Orthodoxy, the Lamb of God is only to be portrayed as a human being—in spite of the strong visual imagery of Revelation. Before crediting such a quick response, it might be good to take a closer look at the evidence.

Wealth of Images

If we turn to the revelatory text, we find that things aren't quite as monochromatic as the critics of expansive language suggest. The variety of images used for God in scripture and in the liturgies and art of the early church is expansive: full of beings animal, mineral, vegetable, and human. Here are a few similes, analogies, and metaphors in these various categories.

In addition to the well-known dove and lamb (Matt. 3:16; Rev. 5:6), the animal kingdom is well represented in the eagle (Deut. 32:11–12; Exod. 19:4) and the mother hen, or at the very least her wings (Matt 23:37; Ps. 17:8; 91:4); or in the more unlikely mother bear or lion (Hos. 13:8). And, of course, in the early days of persecution, the Lamb of God was sometimes ciphered as a fish, as the letters of *ichthys* in Greek spelled out an acrostic for the name and title of Jesus Christ, Son of God, Savior.

It might seem odd to image the source of all life by way of inanimate objects, but God is often referred to as a rock or fortress (Gen. 49:24; 2 Sam. 22:2; and throughout the Psalms); God also appears to Moses and the people of Israel in all sorts of phenomena from burning bush to pillar of cloud or of fire; and in the terrifying thunderstorm or volcanic eruption of Psalm 18:7–14. Jesus refers to himself as gate of the sheepfold as well as shepherd (John 10:7).

The plants are not neglected—recalling that the wheat and grapes transformed by human labor into bread and wine are further changed into the body and blood of and by the Savior himself, and he uses the vine as a metaphor for his relationship with his members in John 15. Paul applies a similar image to portray the Gentile church as a wild olive branch grafted into a Jewish rootstock (Rom. 11:24).

Finally, God is portrayed in many human forms, very commonly male figures such as king, shepherd, friend, and bridegroom; but also in feminine form as a mother (Isa. 42:14; 46:3–4; 49:14–15; 66:12–13) or a nurse (Num. 11:12; Ps. 131:2), and as a midwife or a housekeeper (Ps. 22:9; Luke 15:8–10).

Often the images are placed side by side or even in lists, as if to say, don't get too caught up in these being literal, but make use of them for the evocative power they convey. The Psalms and the Prophets in particular feature the Hebraic use of parallelism—a multiplicity of metaphor and image—quite often paired or tripled images about God: male and female, human and nonhuman. And this is exactly what the new expansive language liturgies are designed to do: not to remove all male imagery, but to supplement it and enrich it with other language. Some examples of such multiple images include:

- the Rock that begets or bears and God who gives birth to Israel (Deut. 32:18–19);
- the father of rain and dew, and the mother of ice and frost (Job 38:28–29);
- a father's teaching and a mother's instruction (Prov. 1:8);
- the master and mistress of observant servants (Ps. 123:2);
- a man of war and a woman in labor (Isa. 42:13–14).

In his own teaching, Jesus continues this practice of parallelism in his parables and often pairs men and women in this way:

- Luke 4:24–27: the widow of Zarephath, and Naaman the Syrian
- Matt. 24:39–41: Two men in a field, two women at the millstone
- Luke 17:34–36: Two men in a bed, two women grinding corn
- Matt. 12:38–42: the men of Nineveh and the Queen of the South
- Matt. 13:31–33: a man sows mustard seed; a woman leavens dough
- Luke 15:1–10: a shepherd finds lost sheep, a woman finds a lost coin
- Finally, not to leave John out of the picture and to provide one last example of long-form parallelism: in John's Gospel, Andrew and the Samaritan woman perform parallel functions of spreading the word concerning Jesus, and both use the same word, "Messiah," in reference to him—the only time the word appears in its Hebrew form in the New Testament (John 1:41; 4:25).

So God can be described in a multiplicity of terms, and the poetic voice confidently states that God *is* all of these things, from "A mighty fortress is our God" (based on Psalm 46) to "I am the Vine" to "God is Love."

The wealth of images from scripture continued to develop in the writings of the leaders of the church, a few of whom felt free to portray

God or Christ in boldly feminine forms. Clement of Alexandria, for example, refers to the faithful nourished on the milk of learning from Christ's breasts (*The Instructor* I.6), and later writers continued this expansive tradition, including Bernard of Clairvaux, Ælred of Rievaulx, Hildegard of Bingen, and, of course, Julian of Norwich.

What's in a Name?

However, it has to be acknowledged that these are images, and "Father" is considered as a "name"—part of a Trinitarian formula not lightly to be tinkered with. This concern has to be balanced with the equal acknowledgment that God is not actually a "father" in the literal sense of human fatherhood—this too is an image for the invisible, a name for the unspeakable.

What, after all, as Juliet asked, is in a name? More simply, as William of Ockham might put it, What *is* a name? There is a delightful play on the concept of names in the ever-humorous deacon Charles Lutwidge Dodgson's work *Through the Looking Glass,* published under his better-known alias, Lewis Carroll—perhaps his playful reminder to us that his name is not what he is called.

> "You are sad," the Knight said in an anxious tone: "let me sing you a song to comfort you. . . . The name of the song is called 'Haddocks' Eyes.'"
>
> "Oh, that's the name of the song, is it?" Alice said, trying to feel interested.
>
> "No, you don't understand," the Knight said, looking a little vexed. "That's what the name is *called*. The name really *is* 'The Aged Aged Man.'"
>
> "Then I ought to have said 'That's what the *song* is called?'" Alice corrected herself.
>
> "No, you oughtn't: that's quite another thing! The *song* is called '*Ways and Means*': but that's only what it's *called*, you know!"
>
> "Well, what *is* the song, then?" said Alice, who was by this time completely bewildered.

"I was coming to that," the Knight said. "The song really *is* *'A-sitting On a Gate'*: and the tune's my own invention."

We might well say, then, that God is *called* "Father," but God's *name* is "I AM" (as revealed to Moses when he asked, Exod. 3:14), but God *is* God. So given the datum that God is *called* "Father," the way in which God *is* Father has to be understood *analogically*, in a way that does not require us—at the same time—to believe, as of other fathers, that God is *male*, which, as we've already established, God isn't. All of our names and titles for God are to some extent *metonymy*—allowing some characteristic of God to stand for the whole, as *crown* can stand for the monarch. The real name of God is, strictly speaking, unspeakable.

So how did God get to be thought of as Father, and to be addressed in that way? What is the source of the attributed but not actual "maleness" of God, and the predominance of this image? Well, what is meant by "Father" is not that God is male, but that God is the *Source*. In Trinitarian terms, God the Father is the one who *begets* God the Son and from whom God the Spirit *proceeds* (leaving aside for the moment the difficulties introduced by those who added "and the Son" to the Creed). Neither *Father* nor *Son* require maleness when understood figuratively, but when some unintended aspect of the figurative seeps over into the actual there is bound to be a consequence. In this case it is natural to form an impression of the one who *begets* as male, even though God isn't male.

The process by which the impression takes hold involves a bit of sociocultural-anthropological reflection. The emergence of the custom or habit of attributing maleness to God is linked with early concepts of natural history concerning the source of life.

First of all, let's back up a bit, digging a little further into human history. Early religion gave a major role to the feminine as creative force, usually in conjunction with assorted male deities. Why? In earliest times, Mother Nature (personified in Mother Earth and Mother Animals) seemed simply to bring forth life. The female was the source of life, bringing forth more life naturally, without male assistance. There is a trace of this ancient belief in Eve's title, "The Mother of all Living."

Eden was the world where God caused all things simply to sprout and grow up from the ground. But the authors and editors of Genesis were post-Edenic and knew that agriculture was necessary, so they did not quite depict Eden as a complete paradise where no labor is needed: man is created to "tend" the garden, even though "God gives the growth."

The rest of the Genesis account traces the development of human culture and civilization. With the expulsion from Eden, paradise comes to an end. The end of Eden brings the movement from hunter-gatherer culture to farming and agriculture (Cain) and animal husbandry (Abel), and with it an awareness of (or rather, a theory about) how life comes to be, and the role of male and female in that production of life, including a shift to the belief that it is *seed* (animal or vegetable) that is the source of life. (Of course, what early humans thought of as *seed* in plants is actually an *embryo*—the proper analogy in plants to human or animal seed is *pollen*.) But this *understanding of nature* marked the decline of the goddess, for she was not the source of seed. The female came to be seen as the vessel for creation and the source of material substance (recalling the root of *material* is ultimately the Latin *mater*—mother).

Early human observers of the phenomena of pregnancy and birth, noticing that menstrual blood ceased with pregnancy, came to think that this blood was being employed as the substance out of which the fetus was formed. As it says in the Wisdom of Solomon, "I also am mortal, like everyone else, a descendant of the first-formed child of earth; and in the womb of a mother I was molded into flesh, within the period of ten months, compacted with blood, from the seed of a man and the pleasure of marriage" (7:1–2). So this was the reigning concept on where babies came from: inert matter is called to life and form in the female through the potent creative energy that comes from the male. It is during this period of human history that the religious world that gave rise to early Hebrew monotheism was formed. God is the source of life, the molder, the shaper, the creator. This relationship is established in the second creation account in Genesis 2, where God "builds" Adam (humanity) out of material from the earth.

It cannot be stated strongly enough how much the lack of knowledge of the real nature of vegetable, animal, and human reproduction (involving both pollen/sperm and egg) shaped the role of men and women in society and in religion. This is not just a notion from the dawn of human civilization: the idea that the male is the origin of the generative force persisted well into the nineteenth century. (Edward Dolnick's *The Seeds of Life* recounts the incredible, and culturally formative, tale.)

So it is that the preponderance of male imagery for God the Creator is a natural reflection of prevailing views concerning the role of men and women, both in reproduction and in society.

This process continued long after the agricultural roots were left behind. What had happened was a gradual symbolic shift in which God was the active, powerful, creative *male* in relation to the passive, fallen *female* portraying the individual soul, the "People Israel," or the church as a whole. The nuptial imagery developed in the Song of Songs, Ephesians, and on through the Middle Ages—Francis of Assisi writes about how the believer, man or woman, becomes a spouse of Christ—derives from the cultural stereotypes that have their roots in ancient agriculture and animal husbandry and the days of the formation of early Judaism.

Block That Metaphor

Now it has been claimed by some that in addition to *Father* being a "name" of God, it is also a metaphor, rather than a mere simile, as the feminine images are alleged to be. There are a few problems with this distinction. First, there is no absolute distinction between metaphor and simile, in the sense that both are analogical (and as we've already established, all language, including language about God, is analogical in that a word *is not* what it denotes). We could say that a metaphor is just an exaggerated form of simile, omitting the comparative *like* and inserting the copulative *is*. The irony is that this strengthens the rhetorical impact of the device but weakens the truth of the statement. When scripture says that "God is a consuming fire" (Deut. 4:24; Heb. 12:29), it is a powerful metaphor, but not a statement of fact. The fiercely monotheistic religion of the children of Israel had no qualms using such strong language as "God is sun and shield" (Ps. 84:11) because there was no fear of thinking this meant that the sun is God, or that God is the sun. Taking metaphors too literally "overthroweth the nature" of a metaphor: and even the most bluntly stated metaphorical declarations lose their meaningfulness when translated from poetic analogy into prosaic fact. Jesus, for example, in the Johannine string of "I am" statements, is asserting various *qualities* of his relationship with the disciples, not that he actually *is* either vine, gate, bread, light, or shepherd in any literal sense. When metaphors are taken literally rather than figuratively, whether in the form of simile or not, they begin to become idols, pointing to themselves instead of to God. God is not any of the things these metaphors state; God is God. God is not in the wind, the earthquake, or the fire—but in the purity of nameless silence (1 Kings 19:11–12). All of our words about God can amount to so much earthquake, wind, and fire, without ever conveying any better sense of God, and perhaps a worse one.

In spite of all the foregoing referring to verbal imagery (an odd turn of phrase to which we shall return in the next chapter), perhaps now is the time to note that physical imagery is foreign to Jewish thought in general. Even physical *descriptions* of people are rare in the Old and New Testaments. Aside from knowing that Elisha was bald, Saul was tall, David was ruddy, and Absalom had big hair (and not a blemish from top to toe), there is little visual description of people in the Bible.

Also note that representational imagery of divinity is strongly forbidden, especially portrayal in human form:

> Then the LORD spoke to you out of the fire. You heard the sound of words but saw no form; there was only a voice. . . . Since you saw no form when the LORD spoke to you at Horeb out of the fire, take care and watch yourselves closely, so that you do not act corruptly by making an idol for yourselves, in the form of any figure—the likeness of male or female. (Deut. 4:12, 15–16)

When we let the verbal male images for God take over, we can slip into the assumption or attitude of holding God as actually male. We need constant reminders that God is beyond such categories and images, that we cannot capture God's being, but only rejoice in God's doing and loving.

The way out of this difficulty is not to take the iconoclastic route that strips all poetry and figure from our liturgies; a course that, if followed to its end, would lead to no imagery or language at all. Rather it makes better sense to enjoy the boat ride, able to refer to and think of the boat as "she" but without for a moment imagining that the boat is actually female. Language—even the revealed language of scripture—is a tool for our use. As Gregory the Great said of worldly goods, "Do not turn provisions for the journey into obstacles to arrival at your goal" (*Pastoral Care* III.26). We can revel in the wealth of images available and revealed to us, all the while aware that they are just that—approaches and pointers to the Divine, but not divine themselves, provisions for the journey but not the destination. We can learn something from the Buddhist teaching about the finger pointing to the moon: the finger is not the moon but only serves to direct our attention to it. The goal is not to come to think of God as female, but to avoid falling into the mental trap that thinks of God only as male. All of the rich poetry and imagery in Christian tradition, all of the wealth of language in simile and metaphor, in parable and sacred story, and—as we will soon see—in art and song—is there as a pointer to the inexpressible and inexhaustible Holy One Who Is. "We may speak much, and yet come short: wherefore in sum, he is all" (Eccles. 43:27, KJV).

Words, after all, *are not* what they represent. That is the whole point of the gracious untruth of metaphor—not actually true but pointing to some truth—that is true of all language. Words are like actors playing a part, whether they strut and fret their hour on the stage, or move the hearts and minds of those who behold them to share the emotion or the idea the author intends. But actors *are not* the character they portray, except in those rare instances when billed as himself or herself. They are playing a part, a role that points away from themselves toward a character, historically real or fantastically fictional. Bad actors are the ones who constantly remind you who *they* are. Acting, like metaphor, is deception that tells a truth. The form of that deception is the issue at hand. The best actors are the ones who make you forget who *they* are as they portray the character who they *aren't*.

And this is more about character than characteristics. There was a time when it was considered normal for an actor playing Othello to take on superficial characteristics, to "black up" for the part, though even by the time Laurence Olivier did so it was challenged as unnecessary. In our time we barely blink at Adams, Burr, and Hamilton portrayed by Latino, African-American, or Asian actors—tacit permission being given for the members of formerly appropriated cultures to have some payback, and to raise our consciousness to the fact that these secondary characteristics are not at the heart of the characters portrayed. Perhaps a time will come when actors will once again be free to emulate those secondary characteristics without fear of offense.

It is the same with our language about God and humanity: we are now in a time where people are acutely aware of how jarring it may sound to speak of God only in masculine terms, and to insist that *man* includes women. Perhaps after a time of exposure to the wealth of expansive language that can point us in a Godward direction, we will once again be free to speak of God as "king" without particularly calling the usual gender of kings to mind. (Recall how Elizabeth I said that though she was a woman, she had "the stomach of a king, and a king of England, too," and reminded her advisers, even at the point of her death, that *"Must* is not a word to be used with princes.") All words, like actors, serve until they retire gracefully from the stage, as all must. The time will come when words of prophecy will fall silent, and tongues will cease. We will someday, as Prospero did, deeper than ever plummet sounded, drown our books—even the Book of Common Prayer and the Bible—for we will be in the presence of the Word, before whom all other words, and we ourselves, must bow.

One Last Lost Coin

This chapter opened with reference to how liturgical language and imagery reflects, but also has impact on, the church's ministry and ministers, in particular how it has sustained the tradition of limiting ordination to the priesthood and episcopate to males. Obviously tradition itself is a preservative, especially in those branches of the church who hold tradition itself in high regard. Even for those for whom tradition is not an explicit guarantor of authenticity, the phenomenon of repetition can form a sustaining force. In this case, seeing only men in positions of leadership in the church reinforces the notion that only men should lead. And seeing is an important part of the process.

Inter Insigniores, the Roman Catholic Sacred Congregation for the Doctrine of the Faith's Declaration on the question of the admission of women to the ministerial priesthood, argues that

> the priest is a sign, the supernatural effectiveness of which comes from the ordination received, but a sign that must be perceptible, and which the faithful must be able to recognize with ease. The whole sacramental economy is in fact based upon natural signs, on symbols imprinted upon the human psychology: "Sacramental signs," says Saint Thomas, "represent what they signify by natural resemblance." The same natural resemblance is required for persons as for things: when Christ's role in the Eucharist is to be expressed sacramentally, there would not be this "natural resemblance" which must exist between Christ and his minister if the role of Christ were not taken by a man: in such a case it would be difficult to see in the minister the image of Christ. For Christ himself was and remains a man. (§5)

Leaving aside the fact that women are as "perceptible" as men, this leads to a kind of sacramental receptionism (in which the believer's perceptions are what render the sacrament valid). This reduces the sacrament from an objective reality into a subjective experience. It also puts an undue focus upon one aspect of the celebrant: sex. Why, after all, should sex be any more determinative of perceiving Christ—even, for the sake of argument, if perception were a necessity for the validity of the sacrament—than any other quality of a priest? And isn't a woman more "perceptible" as Christ than a loaf of bread is as his flesh? Personally, I don't find the figure of a paunchy octogenarian cardinal to be as "natural" or immediate a reminder of Christ as a younger and more ascetical woman.

Which is, of course, my fault. For I should be able to see Christ in every member of Christ's body, for Christ is in them through their baptism into Christ; they are all clothed with Christ, have "put on" Christ—and that one-size-fits-all vestment is the sole perceptible sign that "preaches Christ." It is not Christ's maleness that is of significance, in the Eucharist or in anything else, but his humanity, which obviously includes his maleness, but just as obviously is not limited to or by it.

Which brings us to the lost coin, the theological key and serious doctrine that contradicts the argument that only male humanity can represent Christ. For it is taught that what is not assumed (by Christ in the Incarnation) is not redeemed. And Christ assumed the whole of human nature when he became incarnate as a human being, and the doctrinal proof of this lies in one of the treasures of the Christian tradition: the Chalcedonian Definition of the Incarnation. This definition is found in the Book of Common Prayer, among the Historical Documents (864). It is reflected in the language of the second of the Thirty-Nine Articles of Religion: "The Son . . . took Man's nature in the womb of the Blessed Virgin, of her substance" (868). The doctrine affirms that Christ receives the totality of human nature solely from his mother, Mary, in the virginal conception and birth. And she was, obviously, a woman. You will no doubt notice that this theological doctrine is informed by the prevailing view of the origin of life described earlier: that the masculine life force of divine power uses the feminine raw *mater*ial in a relationship of form to content. The doctrine reflects the belief that human *substance* (and nature) is passed along the female line.

I first noted the contradiction between overemphasis on the maleness of Christ and the Chalcedonian Definition, and the implications for the ordination of women, over thirty years ago. I am pleased to see that some theologians in Eastern Orthodoxy—who hold to the core importance of tradition and take the doctrine of the Incarnation very seriously, while also highly honoring the Theotokos—are beginning to see the implications as well. At an Eastern Orthodox/Old Catholic conference on the topic of women in ministry, scholar Constantine Yokarinis explored and expounded a patristic rationale for recognizing the "Christ-likeness" of women, and how the refusal to accept that likeness effectively undoes the church's teaching on salvation (601–3).

How does this relate to priestly ordination? Let's look at the issue more closely, by asking what relationship sex has to human nature. The nature of any class must be something possessed by every member of that class. But what about sex? "Having a sex" is natural to all human beings. But the actual quality of being male only applies to men; being female only to women; and in a small number of instances, being intersex only applies to those who are, for whatever reason (genetic or hormonal), born with an ambiguous sexual anatomy or identity. So it is part of the manly nature to be male, the womanly nature to be female, which is not to say *masculine* or *feminine*—qualities of *gender* that can be conveyed across a wide range of expressions by any human being. But when human nature is considered as a whole, including all human beings, sex and gender are left to one side, for these are qualities of the individual, as one of many. Nationality, hair color, weight, height, sex, gender expression—all of these are qualities of the individual, and not of the universal human nature.

Therefore, the "natural resemblance" argument already having been defeated both on objective grounds and on the grounds of a proper understanding of the nature of the sacrament, we are left with an assertion that there is something about maleness, as a human quality, that is required for ordination.

And this is where the conflict with Chalcedon arises: for the council affirmed that whatever it is in human nature that is of saving importance (since that is the object of the Incarnation) came through a woman—the Blessed Mother of God—and she could not confer what she did not possess. Therefore, the male character of Christ is not essential to the Incarnation, but—to use the language of philosophy—accidental. Even if Christ's maleness was necessary for the fulfilment of prophecy (as heir to David and King of kings), there is no natural reason to think this carries over to the ministers of the church. To do so is to attach a greater significance to maleness than is warranted.

Many years ago, after much rumination on these debates, I wrote the following in the style of Richard Hooker, based upon the arguments he raised in his defense of women performing emergency baptism; I stress here that these are my words, not his:

> Some say that women may not receive the benefit of the sacrament of order. But how is this; seeing that women may receive the benefit

of both of the sacraments ordained by Christ, and may be, as they will admit, the ministers of baptism, which is the prime sacrament of the church's very being; and seeing that a woman may alike receive the benefits of all the other sacramental rites of the church, in confirmation, penance, matrimony, and unction; wherefore then are they incapable of receiving benefit of this one only rite of orders? Is it that they are incapable of receiving this grace, as if they were a material unfit to receive the impress of a seal? What is the grace? and what that receives it? Is there somewhat in male humanity that exists not in the female? Is it not rather that male and female are qualities of the person, and not of whole human nature? For humanity as a whole is neither male nor female, but each is one or another. To say otherwise were an error, since we know that all that is of human nature in woman comes from man, as Eve was taken wholly out of Adam; and further, all that is in human nature resides in woman, for Christ's humanity came to him wholly by way of his blessed mother, and she could not bestow that which she did not possess: and finally both man and woman come from God as made in God's image (1 Cor. 11:12). So if they say that either humanity or divinity is the form or image that a woman cannot possess, they are mistaken, for she has the first by nature of birth; and further by the grace of baptism whatever of the divine image is marred or obscured in her is restored to its original likeness. Finally, we hold that the grace of the sacraments comes not from the ministers who perform the rites associated thereunto, but from God; and that the lawful performance of a sacramental rite assures us of its validity and of the grace imparted thereby.

So it is that the lost coin, the key to a defense of what some see as a bold innovation, or departure from tradition, rests at last on a careful attention to one of the most ancient doctrinal traditions of the Christian faith: the Incarnation of Christ, born of the Virgin Mary.

4

Behold Who You Are

The Icon as Sacrament of God's Presence

Then God said, "Let us make humankind in our image, according to our likeness." (Gen. 1:26)

We have thus far been making some efforts in *theology*—which literally means "God talk." Sometimes we find ourselves at a loss for words, and indeed I have stressed that words may not be the best or most immediate way to theologize. Saint Anselm long since defined theology as "faith seeking understanding," and you will notice what comes first. My supposition is that you would not be reading this book if you were not already a person of faith seeking understanding. Putting faith to work in seeking a better understanding of God is part of the church's task—its mission.

Of course, as I've also tried to articulate up to now, the limit is that God is so much bigger than the measure of our minds, as the old hymn says. This is what "incomprehensible" means, after all—too big to fit into any of our boxes, or indeed any box at all however big. Yet the quest goes on, and the faithful continue on the journey that all true lovers know—the pilgrimage to come to know "the other" whom we can never know quite as well as we might like, but to and with whom, through continual love and in constant companionship, we daily grow closer. It is good to be reminded that if we can never completely know even another *human* mind, we cannot hope completely to know the mind of God. But still, we love.

In that love, human and divine, we will more often than not find ourselves tongue-tied and at a loss for words, and so I want to reflect on one of the wordless forms of contemplation I mentioned in an earlier chapter. This form is one of the means of visually oriented prayer, taking its place with contemplation of nature and the mandala at other apexes of a visually contemplative triangle. It is the icon.

I began to work with icons as an artist decades ago, inspired by Father John Walsted, formerly a monk of the Order of the Holy Cross, who later served as a priest well into his retirement from full-time parish work, for a ministry of over fifty years. In his very active misnamed "retirement," he devoted almost all of his time to iconography—to such an extent that he often needed to rest his arm in a sling. He had many regular students, and though my own study with him was less formal, I am grateful to him as a guide and inspiration. I have found painting icons to be a valuable spiritual discipline, in particular as a form of heart-prayer that helps me get a bit out of my "head." In prayerful engagement with the materials that make up the icon, I encounter the incarnational physicality of matter being transformed into a reflection of the spirit. And while there is a devotional *askesis* (an ascetical exercise or discipline) in painting icons, as there is in their contemplation, in these comments I will focus on the latter since it is available to many, while few have the time to devote to the former discipline—though iconography has become a popular spiritual exercise, and workshops and retreats take place all around the country.

First, however, a short parenthetical comment on vocabulary. You will have noticed that I wrote of *painting* icons rather than *writing*. This is one of those little details by which people can become pinned and distracted, missing the paint for the brushes, if not the forest for the trees. The long and the short of it is that the Russian and Greek words for *writing* are also used for *painting* (when speaking of fine art, not fences), and it is unnecessary to overemphasize anything distinctive along that line when applied to icons. There is quite enough about icons to separate them from regular secular art without giving their creation any special name other than *iconography*.

BACKGROUND

Let me begin with a *very* brief capsule history of this tradition. Volumes have been written on this subject, and I will only summarize a few of the most important points before moving on to the theological and devotional significance icons have for the life of the church.

The tradition—and tradition is key to understanding anything about icons—says that the first icon was "made without hands." It was a miraculous handkerchief sent to the King of Edessa, portraying the face of Christ, much like Veronica's veil, on which, as Julian of Norwich said, "he portrayed with his own blessed face when in his hard passion, willingly going to his death" (10). Whether these handkerchiefs actually were miraculous or crafty, they served the purpose of a miracle in creating faith. Among the first icons to appear were those replicating the original purported to have been other than handmade.

The hand-painting of icons began very early and may have grown out of the tradition of memorial art and tomb painting. If you've seen the early Roman paintings from Pompeii (I don't mean the naughty ones) or the funerary paintings from the catacombs or Faiyum in the Egyptian desert, you will perceive an immediate similarity to the style of the early icons such as the Christ of Mount Sinai—the large, limpid, haunting eyes and a relatively naturalistic style—before later stylization began to take root as rules were set in place that tended to discourage naturalism.

One aspect (quite literally) of icons persisted from the very beginning, even after other rules were set in place: the figures in an icon look out at you, engaging you with a stare that, while unemotional, is far from blank. Unlike Western religious art, which came more and more to portray or evoke the emotions, the icon was meant to present the faithful with the *person* him- or herself. The saint or figure of Christ stands face-to-face with the one contemplating; it is as if you were regarding each other through a window into heaven, or, as I will expand upon in a bit, as if in a mirror.

Another difference between the icon tradition and Western art has to do with originality. The iconographer does not see herself as a creative artist making something new, so much as a *performing* artist carrying forward a tradition. The icon is a "work" of God in the same category as the Daily Office. Iconography is rather like the performance of a piece of music someone else composed, perhaps long ago, but which makes that past reality come to life in the present. Like the timeless daily repetition of the course of the Psalter, each icon is an instance, not of the artist's *individual creativity*, but of her *communal fidelity*. It is, moreover, like the Office, an act of prayer in itself.

Occasional innovations (perhaps it might be better to call them "developments") do come along, even within the fairly rigid rules laid down by the Eastern Orthodox, so that one can speak of different "schools" of iconography. The durability of tradition, however, is such that once one becomes familiar with them, one can often recognize, even without the labels showing the saint's name, that this is an icon of John the Baptist, that one Saint John the Divine, and that one Peter the Apostle. And given the antiquity and strength of the tradition, one begins to wonder if, after all, these icons may not preserve, even at this far remove, even with the mix of stylization and the variable skills of the artists, an accurate record of how the saints may actually have appeared.

While the tradition has dominated in the East, in the West, where iconography has experienced a rebirth in recent years, the relatively greater freedom of the artist that is part of our culture has made its contributions, and new schools of iconography are emerging and new saints are being portrayed. (I confess that some innovations give some among our Orthodox siblings the absolute willies, but I believe that the Holy Spirit continues to provide an impetus for the new creation, as well as replication of the old. Someone, after all, had to be the first to produce any given prototype either from life or under the Spirit's guidance.) I take some blame and criticism for this in my own iconography, in particular as I prefer a more naturalistic style in an effort to relate to the saints as "real people." In doing so, I believe I am faithful to a more basic *theological* point in the icon tradition, opposed to any tendency to Gnosticism (that denies the goodness of material reality) or Docetism (that denies the full humanity of Christ, implying he only *appeared* to be a real human being), and in keeping with the Orthodox rule requiring the Lamb of God always to be portrayed *as* human. I understand naturalism in this case to be an affirmation of the Incarnation as *real*. Matters of style aside, the important thing about icons is that they are not meant to be admired merely as artistic creations. An icon is far more than that.

FOREGROUND

This brings us closer to the iconic window frame: the theological significance of icons *as they are venerated* in the worship of the church. The creation of an icon is a form of prayer and worship, but so is the act of beholding the icon, in contemplation and meditation. Indeed, the test of an icon, as one Eastern Orthodox archbishop put it, is that it *causes you to pray*. How that prayer is evoked is at the heart of the icon's meaning.

I want to begin by addressing the word *icon* itself, for the Greek word *eikon* does not only apply to a painted panel with a portrayal of a saint. It is the word used for any *image*. Most importantly, it is the word used in the Greek translation of the Hebrew Scriptures, with which Jesus, his disciples, and the citizens of a by-then thoroughly Hellenized (and largely Romanized) Palestine would likely have been familiar. It appears in the passage from Genesis about humankind being made in God's *image*. (For those who think Jesus and his disciples may not have been current with the Greek language in use in trade and commerce in "Galilee of the Gentiles," the Aramaic and Hebrew for *image* are also cognate, so Jesus echoed the language of Genesis in whatever language he spoke.)

And what that first chapter of Genesis tells us is that God, the supreme artist, as the crown and finishing touch of the masterpiece of creation, effectively signed the painting by placing into it a visible reminder of whose work it was. When you want to find out who painted a painting, you usually look down into the lower corner to find the artist's name. But God, when *signing* the creation, put the sign and signature right in the middle, in the person of humanity, having dominion (not, I hasten to add, domination) over all other creatures. Human beings are the *signature*, the *sign*, the *image* of God; and what Genesis teaches us is that when you look at a person you see the closest thing to God that you can see.

People have always wanted to see God, missing the point that God has left photographs and autographs everywhere around us. As the greatest American poet, Walt Whitman, wrote in *Song of Myself*:

> In the faces of men and women I see God, and in my own face in the glass,
> I find letters from God dropt in the street, and every one is sign'd by God's name,
> And I leave them where they are, for I know that wheresoe'er I go,
> Others will punctually come for ever and ever. (48)

This message is much the same as the message Jesus conveyed to his disciple Philip when he asked Jesus to "show us the Father." Jesus said to him, "Have I been with you all this time, Philip, and you still do not know me? Whoever has seen me has seen the Father. How can you say, 'Show us the Father?'" (John 14:9). The divine image Philip and all of us look for was there all along, seen but not perceived.

There is more to our religion than simply seeing, even more than seeing and believing. The vision is meant to lead us to action; our faith is meant to be put into practice, as we love God, and love our neighbors as ourselves, gazing into what Saint Ælred of Rievaulx called "the mirror of charity."

God has given us each other as signs of God's presence; and God through Christ has told us that how we treat each other, what we do for the least among us, is what we have done for him. As John put it very sharply, "Those who say, 'I love God,' and hate their brothers or sisters, are liars; for those who do not love a brother or sister whom they *have* seen, cannot love God whom they have *not* seen" (1 John 4:20).

Finally, getting back to words, Jesus brings this point home in another way, using the word *eikon* as he addresses the crowds in cosmopolitan Jerusalem on the matter of taxation. Now, a number of recent English versions have at this point chosen to translate the Greek *eikon* with the English word *head* (presumably, given the coin, as opposed to "tails"—but thereby losing the resonant connection with the passage from Genesis, and, I might add, introducing an entirely foreign set of *other* resonances, for *head* is a word with its own theological significance). But *eikon* is the word that Jesus is recorded as using when he asks about the coin, "Whose *image* is this?" And when the people tell him it is the emperor, he says, "Give to the emperor the things that are the emperor's, and to God the things that are God's" (Mark 12:17). And the people standing there would have heard an unmistakable allusion to Genesis and would have remembered just *where* God's image is to be found: impressed on every human being, stamped in flesh and blood, dust transformed by God's breath into God's image: God's *icon*.

So the simple four-letter word *icon* carries a lot of weight. In the Eastern Orthodox tradition, an icon is not simply a religious picture intended to remind you of some saint or other, any more than the Holy Eucharist is simply a memorial celebration for our dear departed friend Jesus. For just as the Holy Eucharist makes Christ present to us in a very real way, in bread and wine and in our hearts as sisters and brothers gathered in his name, where he has promised he would *be* in our midst, so too the icon does not simply provoke a memory, but *invokes a presence* and opens a window into heaven. As Evelyn Underhill writes, the icon

> gives to the pious Orthodox a genuine sense of the Presence of God . . . yet without any risk of idolatry . . . perfectly aware that the icon itself is part of the world of things. It is an object which has been set apart by consecration to be a channel of the supernatural and a peculiar focus of prayer . . . and by its very form reminds [us] that God cannot be represented in his essence but only through his revelation in man. (39)

It may seem strange to us that a panel of wood—coated with glue and plaster, painted in layers of earthly and literally earthy pigment suspended in egg yolk and water—that such a physical thing could become a spiritual window to heaven, a means to participate in the saintly or divine presence, for us to stand, as it were, in the here and now, face-to-face with one who stands there and then in the always and everywhere of eternity on the other side of time and space. But it is no stranger to believe that an icon mediates the presence of heaven than that bread and wine communicate the real presence of the body and blood of Christ.

It is no stranger to believe that an icon confronts us with a window into heaven than to believe that when you look at me, or each other, or yourself in the mirror, or the homeless man who comes by asking for a handout, or the pope or the presiding bishop, or a prostitute barely glimpsed lingering in the shadows at 2:00 a.m., or the senator before the microphones, or the traffic warden at the intersection, or the window washer appearing unexpectedly outside the office window like a

Crucifix, 2018

visitation, or any of the millions and millions of others who walk this earth—that when you look at another human being, you are seeing God's image in flesh and blood.

It is hard sometimes to remind ourselves of this truth. God looks so little like God sometimes. For just as the icon made with wood and pigment and tempera can suffer damage and disfiguration, becoming chipped and peeling, stained with the soot from countless candles, bruised with the kisses of countless numbers of the faithful, so too the image of God in humanity can suffer and be disfigured, so much so that it reaches the point at which we might be tempted to say, "How can this, so degraded, so debased, so barely recognizable as even human anymore, be the image of God?"

Yet even as we say those words, we are reminded of the One of whom *these* words were once said:

> There were many who were astonished at him—so marred was his appearance, beyond human semblance, and his form beyond that of mortals—so he shall startle many nations; kings shall shut their mouths because of him; for that which had not been told them they shall see, and that which they had not heard *they shall contemplate*. . . . He had no form or majesty that we should look at him, nothing in his appearance that we should desire him. . . . As one from whom others hide their faces he was despised, and we held him of no account. (Isa. 52:14–15; 53:2–3)

It was upon such a likeness of the suffering servant—a crucifix—that Julian of Norwich poured out the soul of her contemplation, the image of the crucified and suffering Lord, in whom she could see all of suffering humanity. But nonetheless she could contemplate as well the glorious and transcendent Trinity. The icon—like the crucifix—sums up all of the difficulties the rational or agnostic mind has with the doctrine of the Incarnation, that the Word became flesh—and that *that flesh suffered,* died, and was buried—and was raised from the dead. The icon sums up all the difficulties that empiricists and rationalists have with the notion of a sacrament. But we, as Christians dedicated to that quest, believe that God walked among us in person, and in *persons* still makes that divine presence known, challenging us to love God in and through our neighbors, reflected in the mirror of charity.

We members of the one, holy, catholic, and apostolic church understand the reality of God made present to us in physical things like bread and wine, like a panel prayerfully transformed into an image, evoking our prayer.

As poets from the psalmist to Walt Whitman have said, and as the saints have taught, we live in a world so full of God that we cannot escape God's presence even if we were to try. And for those on the quest in a Godward direction, for those of us who seek the trace of the divine image even where it may be least expected, and who long for a glimpse even of the hem of God's garment or the passing wake of glory, we can join with the psalmist's prayer, "The Lord spoke in my heart and said, 'Seek my face.' Your face, Lord, will I seek" (Ps. 27:11).

Icons are simply one more way to seek God's face, to participate in God's presence, to recognize the unspeakable if not to speak it, to remind us what God looks like, so that when we meet our sisters and brothers in the street, "or in shops, or at tea," in the workplace or even in church, we may treat them as they deserve. In doing this we reflect the love of God, the love that God has for each and every one of us who bears that image. As Julian put it, "Because of the great eternal love that God has toward all humanity, there is no gap in love between the blessed soul of Christ and the smallest redeemed soul" (54). Such is the love of God, and such is the dignity of every human being.

Rabbi Joshua ben Levi taught, "Before every human being there go ten thousand angels, crying, Make way for the image of God!" (Deuteronomy Rabbah 4.4). It is of this love, this dignity, and this truth that icons seek to remind us, speaking an unspeakable truth beyond words. May we always so seek God's face and, finding it, so honor and venerate God's presence with us and among us, the glory of God in the dignity of every human being.

Walt Whitman

The Spirit at Work in Church and World

Jesus came and stood among them and said, "Peace be with you."
(John 20:19)

So far we've been looking primarily at contemplative and linguistic aspects of liturgical life. In this chapter I want to begin to shift to the more externally active and explicitly liturgical acts upon which—among other things—we will reflect through the remainder of this volume. I want to begin by addressing the question, What is the object of our worship? Or more precisely, For whom is worship? In other words, What's the point?

I begin with a passage from the book of Acts, the founding event of the church's liturgical life. It is a long passage, but since the crafters of our lectionaries have so contrived it that the full story is never heard or read in a single sitting either in the Eucharist or the Daily Office, please take a moment to read it through here. To enhance the novelty, I offer it in a free translation rather than one of the standard versions.

> As the day of Pentecost arrived, they were all in the same place together. And suddenly a wild sound like a violent wind came out of heaven and filled the whole house as they sat there. And they saw dividing tongues, like fire among them and sitting on

each one of them. Filled with Holy Spirit, all began speaking in different languages, just as the Spirit gave them to declare. Now, Judeans—devout men of every people under heaven—were living in Jerusalem. Word of this reaching them, they crowded together, confused because each of them heard their own dialect being spoken. Amazed and marveling, they said, "Aren't all of these who are speaking Galileans? How is it that each of us is hearing our mother tongue? Parthians, Medes, and Elamites, Mesopotamians, Judeans and Cappadocians, from Pontus and Asia, Phrygia and Pamphylia, Egypt and Cyrenian Libya, and Romans, Jews and converts, Cretans and Arabians: we hear them speaking of God's greatness in our own tongues." All of them were amazed and at a loss, asking each other, "What could this be?" though others mocked and said, "They are full of sweet wine." But Peter, standing with the eleven, lifted his voice and addressed them, "Men, Judeans and all of you living in Jerusalem, let this be known to you, and heed my words. These are not, as you suppose, drunk; it is only 9:00 a.m.! Rather this is what was said by the prophet Joel: 'It will be in the last days, says God, that I will pour of my Spirit on all flesh, and your sons and your daughters shall prophesy, and your youths shall see visions, and your elders dream dreams. Even on my menservants and maidservants in those days I will pour of my Spirit; and they shall prophesy. And I will give wonders in the heaven above and signs on the earth below: blood, and fire, and smoking vapors. The sun will turn to darkness and the moon to blood, before the Lord's great and glorious day comes. And it will be that whoever invokes the name of the Lord shall be saved.' Israelites, mark my words: Jesus the Nazarene, a man proven among you by God with power and wonders and signs God did among you, through him, as you well know; he—by God's determined and foreknown plan, handed over to lawless men—you crucified and killed. God raised him, loosed from the pang of death, because it was impossible for it to hold him. For David says of him, 'I foresaw the Lord before me, at my right hand so that I would not tremble; so my heart rejoiced, and my tongue exulted; and my flesh will dwell in hope, because you will not abandon my soul to Hades, or let your righteous one see corruption. You made me know life's ways; you will fill me with the gladness of your face.' Brothers, I may say of our patriarch David with confidence that he died and was buried, and his tomb is with us up to the present day. Being a prophet, he knew God swore an oath to him that one of his progeny would sit on his throne. Having foreseen this, he spoke of the resurrection of Christ, saying he was not abandoned to Hades, nor did his flesh know corruption. This very Jesus God raised up, and of that we are all witnesses. Having been exalted to the right hand of God, and having received the promised Holy Spirit from the Father, he has poured this out, as you see and hear. For David did not go up to the heavens, but says, 'The Lord said to my Lord, "Sit at my right hand, till I make your enemies your footstool."' Certainly, then, let the whole house of Israel know that God has made him Lord and Christ, this very Jesus whom you crucified." Hearing this was like a stab to the heart, and they asked Peter and the other apostles, "Brothers, what should we do?" Peter told them, "Repent and be baptized, each of you, in the name of Jesus Christ, for the remission of your sins; and you will receive the gift of the Holy Spirit. The promise is to you, and to your children, and to all who are far away, to all whom our Lord God calls." With many other words he testified and persuaded them, saying, "Save yourselves from this crooked generation." Those who welcomed the word were baptized, and on that day about three thousand souls were added, and they continued in the apostles' teaching and fellowship, the breaking of bread and the prayers. And awe came to each soul, as many wonders and signs were done by the apostles. All believers were together and held all things in common; and they sold their possessions and property and distributed the proceeds to everyone as they had need. Every day they continued in full accord, in the temple, and breaking bread at home and sharing food with glad and sincere hearts, praising God, and with the goodwill of the whole people. And the Lord added to their number, day by day, those who were being saved.

That's some story, isn't it? It is amazing what the Holy Spirit will do when people allow themselves to be set on fire. Of course, Anglicans have a notorious resistance to such incendiary behavior. I'm sure you know the old joke about the Pentecostalist who finds her way into an Episcopal Church one Sunday and is chastened by the usher when she bursts out with Spirit-filled exclamations. When she explains, "I can't help it; I've got the Spirit!" the usher retorts, "That may well be, but you didn't get it here!"

Yet I do firmly believe, in spite of certain cool pockets of resistance here and there in our Episcopal Church, to say nothing of our Anglican Communion, that Anglicans do not as a whole deserve the epithet "God's Frozen People."

At the same time, it would be foolish not to acknowledge that when the Spirit comes to *most of us*, it is in a less inflammatory fashion. We certainly don't see flames alighting on the tops of each other's heads; we don't often hear each other speaking languages we never learned to speak, or speaking an unearthly tongue of heaven. How, then, *can* we tell when the Spirit visits us? Is there any external ratification that the warmth we feel within truly finds its source in the Holy Spirit?

We might begin by noting that even *with* such externally visible marvels as tongues of fire and the miraculous gift of languages, there were still some there that day on Pentecost in Jerusalem long ago who failed to see the Spirit at work. They thought the source of the disciples' inspiration was due to an entirely different sort of spirit, and their behavior drunk and disorderly. Some, it seems, are not able to recognize the Spirit even when the Spirit's presence would seem to be most obvious. So how, then, *do* we recognize the Spirit?

COMMUNITY

The first sign of the Spirit's presence with us is *community,* for the Spirit *calls* and *summons* us, drawing us together, or rather *back* together: re-membering us as members of the church so that we can re-member God together. This is one of the reasons I wanted to present the whole of the Pentecost narrative: it does not end with the apostles going out to the four corners of the earth with their newfound language skills. Rather it ends with them gathered in an even tighter and yet growing community, one that holds all things in common and, most importantly for my theme, a community that worships together in the temple and gathers in fellowship for the breaking of bread and the prayers.

Community, then, is one of the great markers of the Holy Spirit's presence: for a gathered group of many to be in and of one spirit. There have always been great souls who have gone it alone, great saints whose solitary encounter with God is the stuff of legend and sacred history. I addressed some of this holy ground earlier, in speaking of the fruits of contemplation, which generally *is* a solitary exercise. The saints of yore number among them the spiritual athletes who encountered God flying solo, out in the wilderness, like Moses and Elijah, or the Egyptian Desert Fathers and Mothers, some of them going so far as to live solitary lives in caves or on the tops of pillars, as far away from human society as they could get. And I cannot neglect mention of the great anchored solitaries of the Middle Ages, especially Julian of Norwich, who chose a path not entirely cut off from human society, but one that maintained a clear though porous separation from "the world" and the worldly. There is a difference between solitude and isolation: Donne reminds us that no one is ever entirely *isolated*, that is, no one is "an island"—however separate those in solitude may appear to be, they are promontories of the main body, not cut off from it.

However, unlike such rare souls as Moses and Elijah or the Desert Fathers and Mothers or the solitary anchorites, most of us will not find God in solitude, but in *community*. God does indeed appear to isolated spiritual athletes like Moses or Elijah in a burning bush or a still, small voice. But if *we* are spiritual athletes, it is much more likely to be as players on a team.

Moreover, the Holy Spirit appears to favor the public assembly over the private audience. The disciples were in the same place *together* when the Spirit came upon them, and the Spirit, far from driving them apart, bound them even more closely together by the end of the account. (It was *persecution* that scattered the church; although God and the Holy Spirit made good use even of that, felixing yet another culpa in that wonderful way God has of turning our worst wrong turns into new directions—such is the mystery of redemption!)

The Spirit came upon the apostles not in the midst of them pursuing their own individual holiness, but while they were praying together, for and with each other—it was at that moment the Spirit blew through the windows and set their souls on fire. And in that moment they became, in one way, what they *were* and what they *were meant to be*. A single atom of carbon cannot fulfill its purpose alone, though it has certain characteristics that allow it to fulfill those purposes when joined with other carbon atoms in the form of graphite, coal, or diamond, or with other elements as part of a living thing. So it is that community is the engine that realizes identity, that makes of us what we are and are meant for. And it is in community—from the most intimate community of a loving couple, to the humble gathering of two or three in Jesus's name, to the wide community of the church—that the Spirit comes to us, revealing Christ in our midst, and revealing us, re-membered, as his body.

Hospitality

When Christ is revealed among us, he shows himself foremost as one who *serves*, who before his death washes the feet of his friends, and afterward responds to their betrayal and lack of belief with words of peace, who offers them forgiveness so that they might be able to forgive in turn. This service and forgiveness find their natural home in community. For just as it takes two to tango, it takes two to serve, two to forgive. Service and forgiveness flow *from* community as naturally as dance flows from music, when you simply have to move your feet to the persuasive beat.

So the ministry of hospitality, which combines service and mercy and grows from community, is the second sign and verification of true communal spirit, the second sign of the Spirit's presence: "see how they love one another" is Christ's identity badge for the church, both for those within and for those outside. We will know each other by our love, and others, seeing that love, will know the presence of the Holy Spirit among us.

We see the emergence of this in the passage from Acts, as the concern for the welfare of the group leads to communal sharing of goods, the gracious and fluid distribution of abundance in the direction of need, as natural as waters flowing downstream to be joined in the great sea.

Hospitality, that flow of grace to need, takes many forms: in a parish coffee hour or visit to a shut-in; in a welcome assist with an unfamiliar hymnal; in the round of prayer the convent offers, in which the visiting guest is gently folded in as neatly as a prayer card in a breviary; in an act as simple as an outstretched hand to help someone on the steps to the altar, or as formal as the baptismal rite itself with its welcome into the household of God. Our Acts account ends with the growing household of the church, and we continue to offer a hospitable greeting to each newly baptized person, welcoming them into a dwelling for the Spirit whose building stones are the church's members.

Do you remember the children's game: "Here is the church, here is the steeple, open the doors, and see all the people"? The outside of a church looks like a building, but when the doors are opened, the living, human construction is revealed—as a community. So hospitality is both the *beginning* and the *fulfillment* of the community we call the church. It is the first thing that the church is *for*. The disciples were gathered when the Spirit came, and the Spirit knit them closer together, adding to their number day by day as they worshiped, prayed, and served.

Proclamation

But let's back up a bit. There is something else to note in our account, and this is the part that, because it *does* get read each year, suffers from familiarity. The first response the apostles made to the Spirit's arrival was to proclaim the story of salvation to each other in many languages, so that those outside the house were attracted by the sound and were astonished to recognize their mother tongues, the languages of their first birth. That recognition would lead some three thousand of them to the second birth of baptism, incorporation into the body of Christ. Thus the Holy Spirit of God sets Babel on its head. Those who in ancient days *didn't* want to be scattered, who made their own city's survival the be-all and end-all of their efforts, who assaulted heaven with a proud tower so that they might *make a name* for themselves, were given the curse of tongues to *divide* them. But on Pentecost, the gift of tongues serves to do exactly the opposite. It undoes the fragmentation of Babel and calls people back together from the four corners of the earth. The Spirit graciously runs the film backwards so that all who once were scattered are now called back together through this same multiplicity of language, not to make a name for themselves, but to give honor, praise, and glory to the one Name under heaven and upon the earth by which we are saved, and to take on that Name in baptism; not to build a tower as an anchor for self-generated human unity, but to find salvation in the strong tower of Jesus Christ, lifted high to draw the whole world to himself.

So on that day of Pentecost, the Holy Spirit gave the gift of language to the gathered apostles. And of course, what they said is as important as the languages in which they said it—the medium was not the sole message, though it served to catch the ears of the visiting multitudes. But it was the *proclamation* of God's saving deeds that ratified the Spirit's presence, a powerful sign of God being with those who spoke. The children of Israel knew this well, that the *proclamation* of the saving story is a constituent part *of* the saving story, and they were always telling that story to each other. Even in captivity, even when they complained they couldn't possibly sing a song of Zion as their captors demanded, their very confession of incapacity to sing became itself a song (Ps. 137), a chorus of memory to fallen Jerusalem, a making-present of Zion even by the waters of Babylon, a warning to their captors of coming judgment, and a recollection and new chapter in their story. And their story sustained them through that exile and captivity in Babylon, that antitype of fabled Babel, and it supported them and held them together through and beyond the destruction of the Second Temple, and even up to this day, through and beyond the most terrible and single-minded effort to exterminate them since they were formed by God as a people.

The proclamation of the story of salvation, what we might call the Haggadah of Israel, has been the spiritual life stream that has preserved this people. The Christian church's story is added to theirs, a supplement and not a replacement, and each of us has a story too, like footnotes and annotations expanding the history of salvation—so that the whole world could not contain the books that might be written.

RE-MEMBERING

However, "the world" that confronts us today is a world where community is shattered, dismembered, unremembered; a world that doesn't know how to serve; a world that has forgotten its own story. The world will not stop talking long enough to hear the gracious possibility offered to it.

Well, the world needs a wake-up call. And the responsibility to give that call falls on us, the members of the church, the body of Christ: to re-member, to welcome, and to tell the story of salvation to the world.

Every Christian community—every parish, every religious order, every prayer fellowship, every outreach group—can be an icon of community, hospitable service, and proclamation. By faithfully gathering as the fellowship of the apostles gathered, by faithfully praying as the apostles prayed, by faithfully continuing to break the bread of life day by day and week by week; by opening their doors in hospitality so that starved souls can flee the plenty of the world for a time and feed on that seemingly sparse but truly abundant bread of life; by sharing the goods of the world for the good of the world, especially with those who have less; by telling the story faithfully to each other, and to all who have ears to hear: by doing these things the parishes and communities and groups can be focal points for the Spirit's action, tinder for the sparks to light, ground for the Spirit to shake and rock the world to its foundations and recall worldly humanity to its true identity.

If all who are pledged to do so faithfully continue to proclaim that story, the world might stop its chatter for a moment and overhear: that's how it worked on Pentecost, and it can work again. People who have forgotten that they are God's children, in the midst of the bustle of great and terrible cities, in the sometimes desperate and lonely quiet of the countryside, in the coldly subdivided patchworks and culs-de-sac of the suburbs—people hungry for God's word might suddenly hear a voice speaking a language they haven't heard for a long, long time, but which they recognize at once: a language from home, reminding them who, and *whose*, they are.

We who are pledged to welcome the stranger as we welcome Christ can open our doors and our hearts and welcome them in, and in so doing we will be magnified, and together we will offer glory to God such as never yet has rung from the corners of the world where God has been pleased to plant us.

If we who are pledged to the common life in Christ can truly live into the spirit of community that finds its home in the very heart of the Triune God, we will by the Spirit of God send forth from our communities such ripples of grace as will echo through the dismal alleys of the cities and over the rolling hills of the countryside, and sweep aside the neatly subdivided principalities of the suburbs.

The Spirit reveals Christ's presence in the gathering of the community, in the service and hospitality that they share, and in the telling of the greatest story ever told. But the Spirit also reveals Jesus to us through a fourth sign unlike any other: in broken bread and a cup of wine. I will reflect on this wonderful gift at greater length in a later chapter, but I would not be true to my text if I omitted at least a passing reference to it here and now. It is in the breaking of the bread, in the fourth sign of the Spirit's presence, in the eucharistic feast, that the servant reveals himself to be the bridegroom, the guest reveals himself to be the host, the stranger met wandering alone on the open road is shown to be the heart and soul of all community and fellowship. And the story takes a classic and surprising turn: like Richard the Lionheart casting off his pilgrim's cloak to reveal the king's bright red cross on his chest to an astonished Robin Hood and his band. And suddenly, all who are present drop to their knees. The king has returned!

Suddenly, though the doors be locked, we realize who has been standing among us all this time, and we can hear his breathing. Suddenly the Holy Spirit descends upon us and upon these gifts, and we remember and are re-membered into the body of Christ, and in this act re-member God.

Once one special Pentecost, the Spirit gathered the apostles together like a harvest of grain once scattered on a hillside. And gathered together they served and proclaimed and feasted. The many were one in fellowship, in the breaking of the bread, and in prayer and service. We, their successors, can do no less, especially given our baptismal commitment to this precious ministry. This is, after all, our *liturgy*, our *work for and as the people of God*. This is what worship is for; this is *who* worship is for. We have been called together and consecrated for a purpose: Christ our Passover is sacrificed for us, and the Holy Ghost our Pentecost has come to us. So come, let us welcome; come, let us proclaim; and come, let us celebrate the feast.

Gregory the Great as patron of church musicians

6

When in Our Music

Feathers on the Breath of God

> Who sings prays twice. —attributed to Augustine of Hippo, but also to Martin Luther

Music has formed a part of human ritual and worship for as long as humans and their music have existed. No culture that we know of lacks music, though a few have attempted to outlaw or abolish it, along with visible images, as unworthy of God or as perils to human faithfulness. The oldest forms of music—vocal melody and percussive rhythms tapped on wood or stone or one hand clapping against another—arise in the first place from the literally spiritual part of human beings, the breath; and in the second place meld with the division of time into repeating intervals and patterns, markers and indicators of consciousness itself, powered by the insistent beating of the heart. There is something magical about music, and it is a close cousin to the miraculous, linked with the source of life.

The archaeological record shows that in addition to tools and weapons, our ancient ancestors took the time to craft bone and bamboo flutes, and without doubt gave voice to rhythm and song long before those first instruments were played. *Homo habilis* was also *homo ludens*—crafty human was also no doubt playful human, and some of that play was musical.

Any doubts about the role of music in prehistoric worship (whatever form it took) are dispelled with the arrival of the historic record, which in all places shows evidence of music, sung and played; images of musicians playing pipes, strings, and drums adorn papyrus scrolls and bronze vessels from the dawn of history. If we expand *music* to include the allied art of poetry (and surely these are siblings if not spouses), then the awareness of the power of *shaped vocality* presents itself in ancient hymnody and sacred song: to the sun, the moon, the powers of nature—and then in due time to the God of Sinai and Jerusalem, eventually understood as the Triune God of whom angels sing eternally. As we will see of architecture in the next chapter, so too with song: human worshipers have long felt that they are keeping time with a choir up above, participating in a universal worship not bound to earth alone, voices natural and supernatural joined in constant praise of the one who gives them breath and life.

Saint Augustine is often quoted as having said, "The one who sings prays twice." What he actually wrote, in his *Commentary on the Psalms*, is not nearly so epigrammatic, but perhaps more meaningful:

> Hymns are songs containing the praise of God. Praise, if not of God, is no hymn; God's praise, if not sung, is no hymn. A hymn must be three things: praise, of God, and sung. Whoever sings *praise*, not only praises, but does so with gladness: whoever *sings* praise, not only sings, but loves the one sung. Praise is the proclamation of one confessing, singing the affection of one loving. (72.1)

And isn't that the marvel of hymnody, that it wraps up all of these elements of praise, prayer, and proclamation in a lovely and loving container? For all the effort spent on academic theology, and in spite of its value, isn't there something compellingly attractive about the hymns of the church, the love songs the church sings? A New York theater critic once wrote in a review of a spectacular production of a mediocre musical, "The audience left the theater humming the scenery." People will rarely be sent forth from our liturgies into the world "humming the theology"—but God willing, their hearts will have been lifted by the power of hymnody, the glorious foretaste of heaven that great music can give us.

Which, after all, is the image of heaven recorded in scripture: the lecture room, the debating hall, or the choir of a great cathedral? John the Divine's glimpse of heaven revealed plenty of choir space, lots of singing, but not a pulpit in sight. Music, bringing with it not only the richness of melody and texture, but the deep awareness of time, pattern, and rhythm; hymnody with its interplay of meter and rhyme, and all the craft of poetry and language—these liturgical arts lift us beyond the level of mere meaning into the realm where the emotions and attention are engaged to give embodied glory to the one who is the rhyme and reason of the universe, its breath and its rhythm and its measure, and whose body, on earth, we are.

SOLO, CHORAL, CONGREGATIONAL, AND INSTRUMENTAL

Music has played a long and fruitful role in worship and liturgy, and the history of its use is equally complex. Rather than attempt to expound that entangled history, I will instead look to the musical forms and performers embodying the separate lines of what amounts to a grand fugue. This approach allows us to see the virtues of the various forms and styles, and their weaknesses, when implemented as part of a community's worship life.

The solo singing of sacred texts, in private study and public liturgy, has an ancient pedigree. Jewish boys (and more recently, girls) have learned to sing the text of the Hebrew Scriptures, following the cantillation symbols (also known as *trope*) that mark the text and indicate both syntax and accent. Of course, this sort of practice is not unique to Judaism, and Buddhist, Hindu, Islamic, and Christian texts are also chanted according to pointing systems that were among the first written forms of musical notation in their respective cultures, bare jots and tittles tucked around the text. This singing serves two functions: learning and proclamation. Any child who has sung the "Alphabet Song" (to the twinkling tune upon which Mozart composed a suite of variations) knows that music can assist memorization. This solo chanted music is not always quite so simple as that, or so simply pedagogical. Some of it grows by elaboration into full-blown melody, often of astonishing and transporting beauty. That same Mozart once said that if he had written the melody for the beautiful solo chant, the *Exsultet,* sung at the lighting of the Paschal Candle at the Easter Vigil, he would never have had cause to write anything else.

For the purposes of proclamation, singing can help a person not skilled or trained in public speaking to become aware of her breathing and support, intonation, and articulation. This serves well for those proclaiming the lessons and gospel, for the preface to the Eucharistic Prayer, and for longer texts such as the Passion Gospel, chanted during Holy Week. While the prescribed melodic turns used to indicate the syntax and shape of the text—marking phrases and forms such as questions—assist the chanter in delivery, they can also help the hearers follow the flow of meaning even if they miss the occasional word. Many of these musical chants also clearly indicate the end of the passage, at which point a congregational response may be expected.

This leads to the next form that liturgical music takes: the call-and-response between a solo chanter and a congregational chorus. This was an ideal form for worshiping communities prior to the wide availability of printed texts, as it was easy for those responding to the cantor either to repeat an echo of the leader's phrase, or to respond with a set refrain; it still serves that purpose well even where books are at hand, and certainly where they are not. This responsorial form reveals itself in some of the Psalms, and in the various litanies that find a place in our present worship, in dialogues as simple as "The Lord be with you / And also with you" or as imbued with meaning as the *Sursum Corda*—"Lift up your hearts"—leading to the Sanctus.

The downside of cantorial singing lies in the tendency to edge over into performance rather than devotion. Ironically, this has happened with the ministry of "song leader" in many Roman Catholic parishes: rather than *leading* song, the leader becomes a soloist. Part of this is a result of posture and position: the song leader *looks* as if they are giving a concert, on a raised platform with a microphone in hand or before them. This does not encourage participation and can convert the congregation into a passive audience rather than a worshipful gathering.

Of course, this transformation can also happen when a choir—particularly a trained and professional choir—dominates worship; instead of supporting congregational singing in addition to its own contribution to the aesthetic atmosphere of prayer and holiness, it runs the risk of turning the liturgy into a concert. To paraphrase Jane Austen's comment about someone wanting more conversation and less dancing at a ball, one might say to those who want more choral singing, "It is much more entertaining, I dare say, but it would not be near so much like a liturgy." Performance mode (or mentality) can sometimes be subtly encouraged in parishes built along the monastic model, with the choir placed between the congregation and the sanctuary, rather than in a rear gallery where their voices support the congregation and they are not quite so visibly appearing to be "on stage."

Still, this is not to say that choral music cannot hold an honored place in worship—far from it, as choral anthems and meditations can provide soul-stirring inspiration and allow the hearers a moment of transcendent appreciation. But such music can also suffer corruption. It is surely ironic that one of the most beautiful of all sacred compositions, Gregorio Allegri's *Miserere*—composed to be sung only in the Sistine Chapel in Holy Week—aroused a cloak-and-dagger effort to obtain a transcription rivaling the theft of silkworms from China. When the sacred becomes a commodity, an object of intellectual property theft, something has gone terribly wrong.

Choir ascendency in worship is at its least helpful when it completely usurps or supplants the role of the assembly, the people of God, in speaking or singing their proper responses; a wise liturgical planner will pay heed to the rubrics and distinguish between a text that "is sung" (without specifying who is to sing) and a text designated for the "Celebrant and People" or the "People" alone. Congregational silence is particularly ironic when a concert mass–setting robs the congregation of its part in the Sanctus, specified in rubric and text alike as "joining our voices with Angels and Archangels and with all the company of heaven."

And it is with this reminder that I turn to congregational singing. There are few more uplifting worship experiences than joining a large congregation singing a well-known hymn with a stirring accompaniment. But hymnody is not the only place where the members of the assembly can join their voices in praise or prayer. The congregation plays its part in the litanies and responses, the music of the ordinary—from the Kyrie through the Agnus Dei—and, returning to one of the oldest portions of our worship tradition, the singing of the Psalms.

Gregorian psalm tones are, of course, part of Western Christian heritage, though they have fallen into disuse in much of the West outside of the monastic setting. Anglican Chant, on the other hand, one of the treasures of our tradition, remains a popular form. It is based on a type of psalm chant, the *fauxbourdon*, that reached its pinnacle in the aforementioned pilfered *Miserere*. Anglican Chant marked an original simplification of that highly developed style, but soon became so refined itself that it tended to become the purview of the choir, often supported by colorful and nuanced organ tone-painting. In recent years a newly simplified form has been developed that even small congregations can sing with (or without) accompaniment, following the natural stress of the lines of psalmody without the need for marked-up texts.

Another congregational form—the Taizé chant—has seen widespread use, practical for its simplicity and useful in helping the singers focus on the natural flow of their breathing through relatively short, repeated phrases. This minimalist approach, originally conceived for youthful, international, ecumenical gatherings (in which the Latin texts recover their utility as *lingua franca*), provide a meditative atmosphere and can be allowed to fill the physical and temporal space as needed, giving rise, as such reverent repetition can, to a calm and reflective "being present."

However, it is hymnody that serves as the primary form of congregational music in most churches. This can be a mixed blessing. Not all congregations have enough members comfortable with singing to offer support to those less sure of themselves. Some assemblies have the mixed blessing of a few whose enthusiasm is not matched by skill; I'm sure I'm not alone in encountering the gentleman who sings everything in the sub-bass octave, or the soprano who puts the "can't" in *descant*. So, while congregational singing can be uplifting, it can also become a distraction from the true object of worship.

By which I do not mean the pipe organ! This instrument is a venerable part of our tradition, and for many churches represents a significant investment both in building and maintenance, as well as a challenge in finding a capable and devoted musician to make best use of it. The organ can be a great contributor to worship: in prelude and postlude, in meditative music in otherwise silent moments, and in support of singing by choir and congregation alike. But it can also come to dominate rather than support, if the musician is not herself a person with a spiritual sense and discipline beyond mere musicianship. Sometimes churches "get what they pay for" in treating organists as if they were mere extensions of the instrument, hired hands there to churn out a product rather than to join in the prayer and praise through the expressive skill they provide.

So it is that all of these forms of music can support and enhance the liturgical life of a congregation; but each also has its downside and can disrupt worship as well as enhance it.

A Word about Texts

Some texts of the liturgy literally cry out for music: few things can sound as flat and dreary as a spoken *Sanctus*; one ought not join voice with the heavenly choir in a mere recitation of the words of their song. The Psalter is clearly meant for singing, though at least here the strength of the poetry, and the fact that the parallelism of its poetic form survives in any language, makes it resonant even if only spoken.

Many hymns, however, would fall flat as distinctly second-rate poetry were it not for the music to which the texts are set. Music can redeem texts, rendering them acceptable and accessible, even when some might otherwise reject the plain text. A case in point is the text of Eucharistic Prayer C in the 1979 Book of Common Prayer. Dubbed the "*Star Wars* prayer" because of its reference to galaxies and suns, this prayer often suffers disuse, perceived by some as trendy seventies eco-awareness. However, even some of those who dislike the text can find it acceptable when sung to the Russian Orthodox chant arranged by David Simmons, ObJN, after Richard Proulx. In this setting, the profound imagery of this text comes to life, and the few words that some find problematical are quickly forgotten.

The downside of music's power to redeem texts is that some texts are actually less worth redeeming, theologically suspect for good reason. One can sing texts that barely preserve orthodoxy, or may even be capable of erroneous construction, without noticing the problems introduced when the poet who penned the words needed to sacrifice doctrine on the altar of rhyme or meter, poetic license perhaps edging over into poetic malpractice. Beyond the syrupy self-centered piety of some hymns, there are truly problematical phrases here and there even in otherwise sound compositions, such as Charles Wesley's "Hark the Herald Angels Sing." This well-known hymn includes the unfortunate clause "Veiled in flesh, the Godhead see"—which could be read as portraying the flesh of Christ as a mere disguise. The poet would have been well advised to stick with the Johannine "Word made flesh." which fits the meter equally well. Of course, even his original choice is immediately redeemed by the following "Hail th'incarnate Deity," to say nothing of the rest of the hymn, which handily refutes Docetism (the heresy that Christ only *appeared* to be human). But even the soundest of theologian-poets can slip when they need to squeeze a syllable or two into a meter or a rhyme.

Another problem arises when musical concerns overtake their supporting role, as when crafting texts to fit preexisting tunes. In current debates on inclusive language, the wording of the *Sursum Corda* ("Lift up your hearts") in the 1979 Book of Common Prayer has come under scrutiny. Some have proposed changing the last line from "It is right to give him thanks and praise" to "It is right to give *our* thanks and praise." Some feel this is an unwarranted shift in focus from God to the gathering. But the perceived problem results from the revision of 1979, not the underlying text. The 1928 version avoided the gender-specific language (which was hardly a concern at that time in any case) effectively with "It is meet and right so to do." In Latin it is a simple *"Dignum et justum est"*—and the present difficulty with a masculine pronoun was created by a wish to fit the text to the "melody" (not a melody, but a tone) similar to that used in the sung version of the 1928 text. This is the odd way in which secondary issues can confuse primary matters. "It is right and good" or "It is fitting and right" or some such clause would have avoided the archaic *meet* and been perfectly fine in 1979 and now, with no need for *him* or *our*; and either of these can be set to the traditional tone (which as I said is not a *tune)*, the music serving its role without corrupting the text.

The long and short of it is that in our music God can be glorified, but we are challenged always to remember that the medium is not the message, and that music as a ministry is a servant—as are we all. Bach said it best when he signed off at the end of each composition *Soli Deo Gloria*—to God alone the glory.

A Few Words about Silence

In all this talk of texts and music, I am reminded of a challenge from the first chapter of this volume, and the importance of silence in worship. Some cultures are shy of silence; I dare say our contemporary American culture is one of them, though the evidence shows (in theory at least) that we are more aware of this shyness and more willing to tolerate and gain from silence than some of our forebears.

For example, the classical Anglican liturgy, as embodied in the 1662 Book of Common Prayer, calls for silence only at one point in the whole collection of worship forms: prior to the singing of "Come, Holy Ghost" at the ordering of priests. The first American Book of Common Prayer of 1789 added an additional sentence of scripture to the beginning of Morning and Evening Prayer: "The LORD is in his holy temple; let all the earth keep silence before him" (Hab. 2:20), but ironically soon followed it with another addition, "Let the words of my mouth . . ." (Ps. 19:14). The original opening sentences of the English rite were of a penitential cast, suitable to lead up to the opening confession. William White observed of this addition:

> The two texts placed in front of the other initiatory sentences were designed to give solemnity to the opening of the service; and yet, I do not know whether they may have had an unfavorable consequence not foreseen. The compilers evidently designed to begin with penitence and confession; but we have lived to witness an increasing propensity to begin with a psalm, without any special reference to those subjects. Such a thing never happened, within

my knowledge, before the said date: but whether it was a result of introducing the two texts, otherwise so very proper, I will not determine. Perhaps it would have been better to have them placed *after* the other texts. (McGarvey 97)

In contrast to all of the preceding American BCPs, the current version seems to have rediscovered the role of silence in worship with enthusiasm; it specifies silence on numerous occasions (the rubrics mention it almost a hundred times). This silence is not just idle time, however: it is meant for a purpose. Often, as in the single silence of the earlier rites, the silence is meant to be prayerful; silent prayer at priestly (and episcopal and diaconal) ordination now comes *after* the singing of "Come, Holy Ghost" prior to the Prayer of Consecration (BCP 533, 520, 544). Periods of silent prayer are specified on a number of other occasions, in the various template forms for the Prayers of the People, and most especially in conjunction with the collect, which almost always comes after a period of silent prayer by the assembly, "collected" by the one presiding at the liturgy to offer a conclusion. This is especially and most dramatically so in the Solemn Collects in the liturgy for Good Friday (BCP 277), which preserve the form in all its fullness, including provision for the assembly to be directed to kneel for silent reflection and to stand for the concluding collect in each section of intercessions.

Other uses for silence are also highlighted. Silent reflection is assumed prior to various forms of confession, and silent, reflective meditation is mentioned at the Office of Noonday (BCP 106) and may follow the readings at Morning and Evening Prayer and the lessons in the Holy Eucharist. Compline and the Order of Worship for the Evening both provide ample opportunity for periods of reflective silence. And we are encouraged to take our own sung advice to "let all mortal flesh keep silence" at the climax of the Eucharistic Prayer—the solemn moment of the breaking of the bread.

Finally, let me close this list of silences with the one call for silence which directly concerns music: when an organ is to be dedicated as part of the Consecration of a Church, it is to remain silent until so dedicated (BCP 575).

However, as I said above, there is a difference between theory and practice, between rubric and action. In practical terms this amount of silence is a challenge to many modern congregations who become uncomfortable after even a few seconds, as anxious as a radio producer is about "dead air." If silence is simply a mechanical requirement, ticking off the seconds, rather than a time for truly reflective and contemplative prayer or meditation, it too has failed to serve as intended.

So it is that both music and silence have their supportive roles to play in our worship; both can serve wonderfully, and both can be misused or abused. As the preacher said, there is "a time to keep silence, and a time to speak" (Eccles. 3:7), as well as a time to sing. But let all be done, as Bach reminds us, to the glory of God alone.

The Stones Themselves Shall Sing

Architecture for Glory

> When Jesus into Zion rode,
> the children sang around;
> for joy they plucked the palms and strowed
> their garments on the ground.
> Hosanna our glad voices raise,
> hosanna to our King!
> Should we forget our Savior's praise,
> the stones themselves would sing.
> —James Montgomery, Hymn 480 (Hymnal 1982)

What image comes to mind when I ask you to think about a church building? Is it your local parish church, or some other church you may have seen on a calendar or a picture postcard? Is it as simple as a white clapboard New England chapel, or as grand and fantastic as the Expiatory Temple of La Sagrada Familia in Barcelona? Is it an image from your own memory—the church of your childhood—or something out of popular culture—Dibley's Saint Barnabus? Or is it something more extravagant but less explicitly ecclesiastical, from the gothic style of Hogwarts to a hulking edifice as severe as Superman's Fortress of Solitude? Is it an English country church, a monastic enclosure, a federal or classical edifice resembling the First National Bank of God, or an example of brutalist modernism? Is it isolated in a field by a graveyard, or nestled cheek by jowl in the middle of a block of tenements or upscale boutiques?

Whatever comes to mind, whatever church you conceive or choose for worship—or avoid as not your cup of tea—the building will say something about both the worshipers who use it and the worship they offer, or are able to offer. The old tag *lex orandi lex credendi*—the law of prayer and law of belief side by side in dialogue—might in this context be reframed as "the shape of the building determines the shape of the worship." Or, as a church organist friend is fond of observing, given the dependence of that almost necessarily architectural instrument on the physical and acoustic space it inhabits, "The room always wins." There is a good deal of "feedback" in these rooms—and not just acoustical.

Of course, churches are built by groups of people with firm beliefs already in place, and forms of worship that reflect those beliefs. They often choose to design their religious buildings so as to express those beliefs and encourage and enable those particular worship forms. You can tell what the designers of worship spaces regard as important by "reading" those spaces—and their "text" is often literally plain, in letters carved or painted. Over the doorway to the Greek Orthodox cathedral in my neighborhood one can read the words in all-caps Greek proclaiming it to be "House of God: Gate of Heaven." In this case the capital caption was added later, because the building was constructed for a Methodist congregation that later moved to the suburbs, and the clue to the identity of those original worshipers depended more on the interior as it stood in their day: an auditory amphitheater designed for praise and preaching, before an iconostasis was installed to convert the interior for Orthodox use.

As with the Orthodox and the Methodists, so with almost all others. Visit the Lutheran cathedral in Berlin and you will immediately see what Lutherans of the baroque era thought to be important: the interior dominated by the holy trinity of organ, pulpit, and altar, in that order. Visit a Quaker Meeting just about anywhere in the United States and you will find a simple space with seating either circular or square, enabling the equality of the members to express itself in their openness to any message that might be received and move whatever speaker to expound. Visit your local First Baptist and you are likely to see the principal feature to be a prayer and preaching desk facing the congregation, ready for exposition and teaching, and perhaps for use in the preacher's memo to self: "Weak point; bang pulpit." The big Presbyterian church in town still has its prominent pulpit front and center, with the communion table off to the side. The architecture of these buildings tells you a great deal about the congregations—at least the congregations that built them.

I say that because, as with the Greek Orthodox cathedral I mentioned earlier, sometimes the present congregation is from a different tradition than the one that designed and erected the building. Changes can be made to adapt the space, but there are limits to what a new congregation can do when the stones want to sing an old tune rather than the one the newcomers desire—and the newcomers might even be unaware of how the shape of their liturgy has been constrained by the shape of the building.

Still, whether a congregation is a successor to another of a different tradition, or the first to construct and inhabit a space, the tradition that shapes the ends toward which the building will be used and the shape of the worship therein is a powerful influence and constraint. To give one example: there is a reason for so many Episcopal churches in the United States to position the choir in rows facing each other in an area separating the bulk of the congregation from the altar, sometimes with a rood screen or other division between the congregation in the nave and the choir in the chancel. To those familiar with monastic life, this is immediately recognizable as monastic "choir seating"—an architectural arrangement inherited from England long after and in spite of the dissolution of the monasteries. To be fair, most Episcopal churches built in this style are not quite so divided as some of their English progenitors, where—as in the old monastic cathedrals—the congregation, choir, and clergy are essentially in separate rooms with small connecting doorways, almost as discrete as the division made by the iconostasis in an Eastern Orthodox setting. Adapting such spaces to new fashions in worship may prove difficult if not impossible. The stones will go on expounding the theology of those whose many hews and biting sculptures formed them to suit the original intent of their tradition, and the room will win whatever the worshipers try.

Consecration of Space

In spite of these inconveniences and restraining obstacles, there can be something inescapably compelling about ecclesiastical architecture. People are very attached to their church buildings. There is a deep human need to *locate* and *consecrate* special places for prayer, for worship, for encounter with the Holy—and this has been going on from the beginning, when people not only sought out but decorated caves and caverns in Southwestern Europe as womblike spaces dedicated to, and evocative of, the numinous. Just as liturgy (especially music) is a tool for the sanctification of time, so too architecture is a tool for the sanctification of space, the setting apart of a particular area of holy ground, the erection of a structure unlike the common home or place of trade and commerce, set apart to a distinct and sacred end.

Of course, as with Lascaux's caves or the sacred groves of Arcadia, it need not be a building. The truly pious can find a place to worship anywhere. I once observed a powerful example of this truth. When I served a parish in New York City, I was part of an interfaith clergy group that met regularly for conversation and lunch. At first the group was mostly a mix of Christian clergy—Roman Catholic, Episcopalian, Lutheran, and Methodist—with a rabbi or two for good measure. Although there were two mosques in the neighborhood, no one had yet made a move toward inviting an imam from either—until 9/11. The existing group of priests, ministers, and rabbis quickly realized that such outreach was not just timely, but imperative; and within a few weeks of the tragic and horrifying events of that early September morning, a public interfaith prayer service was arranged. All of the faith groups were represented by their leaders and a good number of members and gathered in the large hall of the local city park recreation center. The only slip in the arrangement came with the realization that the event was scheduled to begin just at the time when the Muslim participants were obliged to offer prayer at sunset. All agreed that they should proceed, and the formal program would follow. Space was made at the back of the large, well-filled hall, and the Muslim participants went about preparing the space by unrolling small prayer rugs in accord with the Qibla, the direction toward Mecca. Now, in spite of the fact that the very secular building was, like so much of New York City, designed on an approximate north-south line along the avenue, these worshipers were impelled by a larger geography: their prayer rugs were aligned not to the nominal direction of the building, but to the actual direction toward Mecca, differing by a noticeable angle from the large room's walls. And I am sure I am not the only one who thought, "These are people who take *space* and its consecration seriously."

They are, of course, not the only ones. Many Christian churches are still built so that the congregation is facing east, toward the rising sun—at least approximately so, and when that is possible given the exigencies of urban planning and the architecture budget. I will say more about this in the next chapter, but flag here the seriousness with which Christians have long held to nominal if not actual adherence to this ancient tradition of eastward-facing prayer.

On Earth as in Heaven

Direction or orientation is only one factor in the sanctification of space, though perhaps the simplest: it can, after all, be as easy as being aware of which way you are facing, and may not even require a building—or a prayer rug. But more often than not, worshipers have constructed more durable structures to sanctify space and provide for their worship, whether of wood or eloquent stone. This reflects, in part, the human desire for a realized eschatology—bringing the completion of all things at the end of time into the present reality of worship, to create an image of heaven here on earth. It can also sometimes serve to express that less admirable human desire to nail things down and capture the ineffable in the permanent—which in the long run is not so permanent after all, as "tower and temple fall to dust" (Hymn 665).

Such was, in part, that early building exercise in Babel. Scripture seeks to downplay and ridicule Nimrod's aspirations by indulging in some false etymology about the babbling confusion of language. But *Babel* really means "gate of God," and that was the exalted but presumptuous intent of Nimrod and his monolingual folk, who made the mistake not of trying to bring heaven down to earth but of trying to climb up to heaven themselves. The real Babel, of course, was Babylon, and its rulers had the good sense to follow the less lofty impulse to recreate heaven—or at least paradise—in an earthly garden that would come to be listed as one of the wonders of the ancient world.

Meanwhile, turning to the holy people of God, it appears their experience in Egypt served as an object lesson in how *not* to build, as the Egyptians' most significant architecture was intended as funerary transport to get the select few putative demigod rulers from this world to the next. No, for a long time the people of Israel rejected any architecture for God's dwelling as much as they rejected images for God, keeping true to the *via negativa* that seems to underlie so much of Torah spirituality: an unseen God who cannot be portrayed in an image, whose Name must not be spoken, and whose dwelling is beyond time and space—but who is content to travel in the meantime in (or more accurately enthroned upon) a gilded wooden box, housed not in a permanent stone structure but in a tent and a tabernacle.

But even that tent and tabernacle—and ark—were, according to the text (Exod. 25:8–9), based on a heavenly prototype and design, direct from God's hand to Moses's. It was only much, much later, after God had rejected David's move to do so, that Solomon gained leave to construct a more permanent structure than the tent and tabernacle that had served God up until then. Of course, when monarchs and politicians engage in building programs, one is wise to suspect some political purpose may lurk beneath the piety as a way to consolidate their power over the worshipers as much as to regularize the worship; Josiah's and Nehemiah's efforts in Jerusalem suggest at least some such mixture of motives; and surely there is no doubt that the reconstruction program under Herod the Great owed more to such desires than otherwise, in the face of Rome, to make Israel great again.

No Temple in the City

This reminder might bring us up short, but it heightens the awareness of the reality that even good things can be used for bad ends: this is the nature of idolatry. There is an architectural equivalent to the aniconic (if not iconoclastic) spirit in the tradition, a reluctance to put too much stock in structures. It is similar to the discontinuity in the biblical tradition between the sacrifice laid out in the Law and God's apparent rejection of (or at least disregard for) such a bloody mode of worship recorded by the Prophets (Amos 5:22, 25) and in the Writings (Ps. 50:7–14). There is a clear tension between the call to build a permanent structure and the willingness of God to dwell as and where God chooses, regardless of previous instructions or human efforts.

Ezekiel, for example, portrays God's freedom to depart (chs. 10–11) or dwell (ch. 43) according to the faithfulness of those charged with the maintenance of the temple, a freedom echoed by Jesus (Matt. 23:37–38). Sometimes, it seems that, as Charles Williams is reported to have observed, "the altar must often be built in one place so that the fire from heaven may come down someplace else" (Lewis, *Letter to Malcolm*, 117).

That "elseness" is expounded nowhere so eloquently as in that simple clause from Revelation, "I saw no temple in the city, for its temple is the Lord God the Almighty and the Lamb" (21:22). God is "all in all" and the locus for all true worship, neither here nor there, but "in spirit and truth" (John 4:21–23).

For just as the true icon of Christ is one not made with hands, but impressed on cloth by his human face, the true temple of God is the temple not made with hands, but the Body of Christ, raised after three days; not the building program of over forty years, but the miraculous reconstruction of a *personal* temple that is both human and divine. For this temple is not just the body of the risen Christ, but the body made up of all faithful people, all of the members of that body, as in the children's verse alluded to elsewhere in this volume: "Open the doors and see all the people." That is the true temple and it is the true church—not eloquent stone, but living flesh.

It is good to remember this lest we become too enamored of our own constructions rather than God's work. For is it any less presumptuous to carve the slogan "House of God: Gate of Heaven" over the door to a church building than it was for Nimrod & Co. to claim their tower was the Gate of God? Perhaps we always need the reminder that we worship God, not our church buildings; the inhabiting Guest pleased to dwell with us, and not the dwelling. The adage "Where your treasure is . . ." serves as a stern reminder to all charged with the maintenance of the church and its patrimonial temporalities, just as we are reminded on Ash Wednesday concerning ourselves, that they too are dust, and to dust they shall return. The stones of our church buildings speak, but what are they saying? Words of praise, or of condemnation? "Look at the state of my disrepair." "This is how these people spend their resources." Do gorgeously decorated Gothic Revival church buildings fulfill Pusey's hope to give the poor of the bleak, gray factory towns of the Midlands a glimpse of a colorful heaven on their Sabbath day, or do they shout to them, "Your sort are not welcome here"?

BACK TO EARTH AND REALITY

This is a sobering message given the state of the church today. Everyone knows that the temporalities of the church can be a burden, both emotional and financial. Take church buildings, for example; and given the weight of that burden I am tempted to add comedian Henny Youngman's "Please!" Given the historic reality of building materials, styles, and codes, churches built in the late nineteenth century usually require major work (such as a roof replacement) after about 150 years, those built in the 1910s and 20s after about 100 years, and those built in the 1960s in about 50 years. We live in an era when the time for repair of most church buildings has come or is now past. As a former bishop of New York lamented to me one day, shaking his head as we walked down the side aisle of the Cathedral Church of Saint John the Divine during a rainstorm, and a sheet of water streamed down a broad section of the interior wall from a prodigious leak in the roof above, "If only we could tear this down and build a normal-sized church!" The iconoclastic temptation can be strong, and its foundations run deep into an authentic strand of piety—and common sense.

But there is another way. Instead, let me look for a more biblical word. When Moses reached the borders of the Promised Land, he said to the people of Israel, "I am setting before you today a blessing and a curse" (Deut. 11:26). As the priest of a parish that had to spend almost half-a-million dollars to replace the roof of its historic landmark building, I can resonate with that sentiment. That historic building is a blessing, but it comes with a cost. Some of us, no doubt, have often wondered what our predecessors were thinking as they built so massively in wood and fieldstone and granite—and as Groucho Marx observed, "You can even get stucco. Boy, can you get stucco!" How many of our ancestors in the church ceremoniously burned the mortgage when the bank loan for the building was paid off, as if that was the end of the expenses involved in its maintenance and care? Dare I ask further, How many lifelong members of some of our churches now find themselves unable to enter the buildings whose continued existence testifies to their faithful financial support, because the impressive stone stairways bar entrance to their wheelchairs or walkers? And what of the very different message Gothic architecture sends to children today? A child once stopped me on the street outside my Bronx parish church, a model of English Country Gothic, and asked if it was a haunted house.

However, at the same time, God reminds us that while there are always difficulties, yet we are called to "give thanks in all circumstances" (1 Thess. 5:18). We dare not see these difficulties as a curse—for if we do, we admit defeat. I was, for example, able to turn that child's question about a haunted house into an opportunity to teach him something about the church, about how long it had stood there, and what it stood *for*. The congregation was able to find the funds to add ramps as needed to welcome members and newcomers in their wheelchairs. The church was able to turn the roof replacement project into an opportunity for publicity and consciousness-raising in the community. If we can come to see our church buildings and the issues surrounding them not as curses but as blessings; not even simply as challenges but as opportunities; and not even only as opportunities but as tools for the worship of God and the mission of the church, the fulfillment both of human hope and divine desire, for the spread of the gospel, for outreach to a spiritually and physically hungry world, then we can begin not only to see the importance of our stewardship and care of these resources but to imagine new ways to adapt and adjust to the changes in the world around us.

There will always be the temptation to jump on the bandwagon of success that some of the nondenominational megachurches appear to have in shaping their worship spaces to meet the needs of generations raised with short attention spans. The question is, will this in the end produce a lasting congregation of mission-geared members or a transient audience of satisfied customers? We Episcopalians are fortunate to have not only a finger on the pulse of the modern world, and the capacity to look to the future, but a rich tradition that reaches back centuries and includes many cultures. This is a great tradition that many parishes have drawn on, recovering the deep spiritual nourishment in ancient practices of prayer and worship. They have found—ironically enough—that Generations X, Y, and so on are hungry for food that will sustain them on the journey, rather than a snack, and are seeking a direction for their lives rather than mere diversion for the moment.

In looking at our buildings and the worship that takes place within them, it will be important to distinguish between tradition and its poor cousins: custom and habit. It will be important, as we look at present and future needs, to challenge the proverbial claim, "We've always done it that way," and in doing so perhaps discover that what we always thought was a hallowed tradition dates back no more than a generation. As Diana Butler Bass says in her study, *The Practicing Congregation*, "In every generation of Christian history, faithful congregations have selected and reshaped tradition, developing patterns that reflect transcendent realities in ways that speak to the surrounding culture" (94). This is challenging work, but it will also be enriching and rewarding, as we dig deep into the wealth of our past as well as make best use of the possibilities of our present: like the wise householders of whom Jesus spoke, who bring out of their treasury both the old and the new (Matt. 13:52). Fully making use of our blessings will require the twin skills of memory and hope—and imagination.

Should the present church leaders and members fail in this, it will likely best be said of them—as New York's Bishop Horatio Potter said in his address to the convention of the diocese in 1872, when he called for the beginnings of that great Cathedral Church of Saint John the Divine—that unless that structure,

> while it presents an edifice and a worship which for majesty, for reverence, for genuine power of religious expression, shall be fitted to represent and set forth the majesty of our Holy Religion, as well as the dignity of our Branch of the Church . . . I say, unless [it] can be so ordered as to be a centre of unity and sympathy and power among us, I, for my part, have no ambition to see its foundations laid during my day.

And so we come back to earth, back not only to the reality of the hard work of stewardship and mission, but all the way back to the earth from which the first human was made, to the *humus* of the *humanum,* the true *locus classicus* of God's image and dwelling. We are reminded not to make our externalities—our temples and towers and all their glorious furnishings—the object of our worship, but to treat them as pointers to the Mighty One whom we will find in the lowliest and the weakest. As Bishop of Zanzibar Frank Weston reminded the assembly at the Anglo-Catholic Congress of 1923, in his stirring address, "Our Present Duty":

> You have got your Altar, you have begun to get your Tabernacle. Now go out into the highways and hedges where not even the Bishops will try to hinder you. Go out and look for Jesus in the ragged, in the naked, in the oppressed and sweated, in those who have lost hope, in those who are struggling to make good. Look for Jesus. And when you see him, gird yourselves with his towel and try to wash their feet.

We are reminded, as the angel Dudley reminded Bishop Henry in *The Bishop's Wife*—like many real bishops such as Potter and his successors, torn by the many competing calls and the limited resources at their disposal, in Henry's case yearning to give glory to God through a great cathedral building program—"That big roof could make so many little roofs."

We are called to count the cost and make the best use of our resources. The stones themselves will speak, to give glory—or to condemn.

TURNED TOWARD MISSION

PEOPLE LOOK EAST

I mentioned in the preceding chapter the saying current among liturgists, especially organists, "The room always wins." One of the more contentious issues of liturgical reform in the last third of the past century concerned the position and posture of the priest and people in relation to the altar and each other. Many exponents of the Liturgical Movement, both in the Roman and Anglican Communions, encouraged the erection of freestanding altars in newly constructed church buildings (the ravages of World War II in France and Germany gave ample opportunity for this) and the relocation of altars (or where impractical, their supplementation with new altars) in existing buildings. Historical and liturgical arguments were invoked in favor of the move toward freestanding altars and celebration in which the priest and people faced each other over and across them. It was commonly asserted that this was a recovery of ancient tradition, and that it fostered a greater sense of the church as a gathered community empowered for mission. However, I join a number of historians and liturgists who find it prudent to reexamine these claims, not just to rearrange the furniture once again (or to resist it) but to think through what our liturgical grammar is saying when we pitch our tent one way or another.

History Reexamined

The part of this literal "liturgical movement" connected with the furniture has some historical basis: altars had, for the most part, been freestanding in earlier eras, based on the scant evidence of the earliest house churches, the well-documented basilicas, and on through the renaissance—and the placement of the altar as a massive sideboard against the eastern wall of the apse was a fairly late development. However, even these high altars of the baroque era, though they appear to be up against the eastern wall due to the elaboration of gradine and reredos, almost without exception have passageways behind them to allow the circumambulation that was the rubical rule in the time of their dedication (Anson 1948, 76). (Such technical compliance with the rubric reminds me of how conscientious Anglo-Catholic clergy would crease the host with the edge of the paten, in deference to the "lesser fraction" rubric of the older rites, saving the complete breaking of the bread for the point at which they knew it to be proper in spite of the rubrics.) So at least as far as historical precedent for the position of the altar itself goes, those advocating it be freestanding had some foundation.

Along with the restoration of the freestanding altar, liturgical revisers encouraged celebration of the Eucharist with the priest facing the people (technically called "versus populum," henceforth "VP"), in the earnest belief that this was the ancient position for the celebrant, whether bishop or priest. However, even during the height of the Liturgical Movement and the Vatican II reform, cautionary voices were raised. Few scholars felt the freestanding altar required or implied a VP celebration, and the primary impetus for change appears to have been the enthusiasm generated in rearranging the furniture. A calm and careful look at the historical evidence undertaken since the heady days of the sixties and seventies has led many to reexamine and rethink the matter.

What the evidence shows is that, with very few exceptions, the celebrant at the Eucharist rarely faced the congregation across the altar, at least during the Eucharistic Prayer. It appears that the position of the bishop's chair behind the altar in the early basilica may have been the source of the confusion. Since bishops faced the people during the liturgy of the word, it was wrongly assumed that they continued to do so at the prayers or at the liturgy of the table. However, the early church was not concerned about whether bishops faced the people or not, but about the direction all worshipers, including the bishop, faced for prayer. Prayer—above all the Eucharistic Prayer—was (and is) addressed, not to the assembly, but to God. The traditional direction for prayer was toward the east, toward the rising of the sun that symbolized the coming of Christ. This meant that in churches that were "oriented" with the apse in the east, the bishop would come around the altar and join the congregation, leading their prayer as they all faced east together.

In the city of Rome, however, basilicas were often if not always "portal oriented"—that is, their entry door faced east, and the altar was in the western end. In this case, the bishop was already facing east for prayer, and the congregation would turn to face east *with him*, leaving the altar behind them. This may seem odd to us, but in this early period the later concern with "seeing the consecration" had not yet evolved. Indeed, in the Eastern Orthodox tradition, visibility was never a primary issue, as the whole people of God, clergy and laity, were quite happy to pray together in the same direction whether they could see each other or not (Jungmann 137f; Bouyer 175). As Louis Bouyer notes:

> The notion that the arrangement of the Roman basilica is ideal for a Christian church because it enables priests and faithful to face each other during the celebration of Mass is really a misconstruction. It is certainly the last thing which the early Christians would have considered, and is actually contrary to the way in which the sacred functions were carried out in connection with this arrangement. (175)

There is no need to rehearse here the process by which the basilican freestanding altar evolved into the magnificent layer-cake sideboard of the Middle Ages, though Jungmann suggests that the impracticality of the people turning away from the altar (in the Roman portal-oriented layout) led to the development of "altar orientation," the notion of a "liturgical east," the movement of the altar deeper into the apse, and the adoption of the "eastward position" (EP) in which the celebrant turns to join and lead the people, facing east with them (138).

It is fair to say that this practical change was accompanied, but not driven, by a developing theology of sacrifice. It was largely in reaction to this theology of sacrifice, and a desire to introduce a resemblance to the "Lord's Supper," that the Reformers transformed the altar into a table around which the assembly gathered—though here too their intent had little historical authority, even if the early Eucharist had ever been conceived of simply as a recreation of the Last Supper. For in a classical banquet all those partaking, host and guests alike, sat or reclined on the same side of the table or tables, waited on by servants on the other side—an image preserved in countless (even late) representations of the Last Supper (Ratzinger 78).

Many of the newly designed freestanding altars of the Roman Catholic tradition in the middle of the last century still required an EP celebration. A number of photographs of these grand but now rather dated "modern" liturgical spaces (even in texts such as Hammond's, which advocate VP) reveal the limitations upon this posture, due to the tabernacle and candlesticks still present on the mensa of the altar. It was only with and after Vatican II that the Roman Catholic Church, by banishing the tabernacle and candlesticks (admittedly late additions) from the altar, made VP celebration almost universally possible, though as some Roman Catholic liturgists are now emphasizing (as they reconsider the wisdom of this change), the rubrics do not actually *require* this posture. It has also been pointed out that even at Saint Peter's, where the pope has stood opposite the people since the basilica was constructed, it was not in order to face them: indeed, in the long period from the baroque until Vatican II the celebrating pope could no more see the people than they him, due to the large cross, candlesticks, and tabernacle between him and them.

On this side of the Tiber (and the Atlantic), our own Book of Common Prayer rubrics still expect the EP posture for the Eucharistic Prayer, as the rubric at the end of the dialogue leading to the preface states, "Then, facing the holy Table, the Celebrant proceeds. . . ." (BCP 361, etc.; note, however, that the mention of posture in the rubric has disappeared from the Spanish version of the BCP.) Bonnell Spencer, writing in 1965, noted that the rationale for the introduction of VP in the Roman church provided a means of improved visual participation in a church which at that time conducted much of its liturgy in a low voice and in the Latin language, but that the Anglican tradition had less need of such visual rearrangements because it had long since dealt with verbal accessibility in its liturgy. Joint prayer of the people and priest together, he remarked, "is a far superior form of corporate participation than merely watching the celebrant" (161). (This may well represent an example of the "verbal orientation" to which I referred in chapter 1, "The Hand and the Jawbone.")

Yet in spite of the shaky foundation for the historical argument for VP, that it represents a recovery of the ancient tradition of the church, it has become the dominant Roman Catholic liturgical fashion, and is now prevalent among Anglicans.

There are times when historical justification is less significant than present need—tradition should inform but not bind the church in its efforts to serve. However, while we need not be dominated by our history, we should at least be well informed concerning it, particularly if we are going to argue from it. Liturgists in particular seem to fall prey to a kind of historical nostalgia, whether for the apostolic, patristic, or some other golden era. But it is no good picking up one feature of some past liturgical customary (always assuming that scholars and fashion-setters have it right—which it seems many didn't with VP) and simply patching it into our contemporary situation. New wineskins really are needed for new wine, and there has been a lot of water under the Milvian Bridge.

COMMUNION AND COMMUNITY

So is there a compelling rationale for VP—or a return to EP—on some other basis than the historical? When making liturgical changes (whether one sees them as a recovery or a development) it is important to consider the whole context of the world as it is today, and what different meanings and effects a gesture from the fourth century may have for us. We really ought to be saying what we intend, with actions as much as words.

My conclusion is that while VP has its place in some environments where the notion of community is particularly strong (especially communities such as convents or schools, or informal private gatherings), it raises a number of practical and pastoral problems, and what is worse, may have had and continue to have deleterious effects on the parish, the wider church, and its understanding of mission and ministry.

Far from encouraging a growth in the sense of community, as texts from the Liturgical and Parish Communion Movements too numerous to list insist, the dominance of VP has sometimes led on the contrary to a new form of clericalism. How so?

Take, for example, Peter Hammond's critique of EP and his insistence that VP not only will bring about greater liturgical participation, but spur the laity on to apostolic mission in the world. (Note as well his acknowledgment that the foundation for VP is ideological rather than historical or, as he says, "missionary rather than antiquarian.")

> Preoccupations that have already brought about a widespread restoration of the ancient ceremonies connected with the offertory and the celebration of the Eucharist versus populum have all been missionary rather than antiquarian. So long as the layman in church remains a passive spectator of something done on his behalf by professional actors, it is likely that he will be equally passive in regard to what is done out of church. (168)

There are a number of logical and historical problems with this assertion. I have already addressed the historical assumption concerning VP itself. Here it is more important to note that the church's great missionary efforts in previous ages managed to flourish without the benefit of VP, and many laity, Roman and Anglican alike, have gone forth from churches with baroque or gothic furnishings and antique ceremonial nourished with a sense of mission and outreach. Nor has there been a notable resurgence of such mission and outreach since the adoption of VP as a virtual norm. One need only cite Jesuit mission and Jesuit architecture to see the first false assumption in Hammond's assertion.

More problematical is Hammond's remark concerning performance. I have actually been a professional actor, so I can assure you that the one thing professional actors are above all eager to avoid is turning away from the audience. While it is certainly true that some priests who used the EP may from time to time have thought of themselves as performers, and some congregants who worshiped in their churches may also have felt themselves reduced to spectator status, that clearly has nothing to do with the professional theater, and any actors who habitually upstaged themselves and turned away from the audience would soon find themselves out of work. Actors quite normally face their audiences, and while there is one time in the liturgy where a certain element of performance craft is not out of place—the sermon—in general any semblance of "performing" should be restrained.

Moreover, VP *enforces* the "performance" mode rather than minimizing it, most particularly in the eucharistic celebration, where the celebrant can be perceived as a kind of ecclesiastical Julia Child confecting the Eucharist behind the table with running commentary addressed to the congregation; or worse, acting out the Last Supper, forgetting that the Eucharistic Prayer is not addressed to the assembly, but to God. It would seem the Reformers may have had their way after all, and the Eucharist has been transformed into the middle act of a passion play. How many times have clergy been tempted (and failed to resist the temptation) to enact stretching out their arms upon the cross or similarly pantomiming the surmised actions of Christ at the table in the upper room? Far from avoiding performance mode, VP has virtually set it in stone, as the altar becomes a barrier as substantial as any rood screen, and as definitive and divisive of the liturgical space as any proscenium is of the theatrical. This has burdened many clergy with the assumed task (in many cases far beyond their talent) of performing for, rather than praying with, their congregation. As with the argument raised in *Inter Insigniores* in defense of the male priesthood, the focus on the celebrant and the congregation's perception of *him* becomes central. It is, in short, a less subtle and more demanding form of clericalism. As Bonnell Spencer pointed out, "Far from being eliminated, the idea that the priest is celebrating for the people is made more explicit. They can watch him do it" (162).

Of course, this model of the priest as *alter Christus par excellence* fits into the Roman Catholic conceptualization of church hierarchy, as an essentially papal model of eucharistic celebration became the norm for every parish (as the suggestions in the General Instructions on the Roman Missal of the 1960s came more and more to be interpreted as rules in the 1990s and beyond). If one wishes to emphasize hierarchy, there are few more effective ways of doing so than dividing the people from the celebrant, one facing many. Note this 1993 instruction from the Congregation for Divine Worship and Discipline of the Sacraments:

> The celebration of the Eucharist versus populum requires of the priest a greater and more sincere expression of his ministerial conscience: his gestures, his prayer, his facial expression must reveal to the assembly in a more direct way the principal actor, the Lord Jesus. One does not improvise this; one acquires it with some technique. Only a profound sense of the proper priestly identity *in spiritu et veritate* is able to attain this. (12:1)

In my experience, clergy more often attain the level of talent-show MCs or nightclub performers; the burden of being a performer is more than most can bear. I will address below at greater length the even larger presumption, and burden, of "revealing to the assembly in a more direct way . . . the Lord Jesus."

Another problem with VP is the loss of clarity concerning to whom the various parts of the Eucharistic Prayer are addressed. EP made it very easy to distinguish those portions addressed to the assembly from those in which the presiding minister turned to lead the assembly in addressing God, normally symbolized (or at least given liturgical focus) through the cross above and to the east of the altar. With VP, the celebrant finds him or herself either looking into thin air or at a stained-glass window at the far end of the building, lowering the eyes to concentrate on the altar book or the chalice and paten, or looking at the congregation (thereby giving the impression that the Eucharistic Prayer is addressed to them). And what does the congregation have to look at? Again, the smiling or somber priest must naturally become the focus of attention. After all, isn't it rude not to look at someone who appears to be speaking to you? The liturgy comes to be more and more *about the celebrant.*

On the mission and ministry front, the widespread adoption of VP has led, not to greater lay involvement in church mission either for Roman Catholics or for Anglicans, but to a proliferation of lay participation in roles on the "other side of the rail," and greater lay involvement in "speaking parts" for the Roman Catholics. (The Anglo-Catholic parish always had lots of things for people to do "on the altar" even if the celebrant had most of the lines.) "Participation" is often assumed to be limited to being a reader, an acolyte, a chalice administrant, or an intercessor, all of them formerly ministries not of the laity but of the "minor orders," and many of them once the reserve of the deacon (and of the many forces working against a revived and flourishing diaconate in our time, this may be one of the most insidious). Often the quest for greater lay participation in the congregation has precisely the opposite effect, as in the Roman Catholic ministry of "song leader" referred to in an earlier chapter—this can have the effect of rendering congregations completely silent as they are "led" by someone who appears to be performing *for* them rather than as one *of* them.

Ultimately, no amount of such "participation" will have an impact on what people do out in the world unless while assembled in church they have been fed with the bread from heaven and transformed in their hearts to become what they behold. Theater on a proscenium stage, or a three-quarter thrust, or in the round, will always have its actors and its spectators, and if what you think you are doing in church is theater, a refined *technique* for *actors*, then it really doesn't matter which way you face.

TURNING ONE'S BACK FOR LEADERSHIP

Many supporters of the VP movement in the last century commonly described EP as the priest "turning his back on the people" (Lowrie 158). This indicates an essentially clericalist focus of concern. No one ever suggested that the people in the front pews had turned their backs on the people in the rest of the nave. For those with this concern, it is the priest who matters, and who he or she is facing. But though it may be true that many clergy who have used the EP think in terms of who they are turning away from, I think many more rightly focus on whom they are turning toward as they join their congregations to face the same direction together. Liturgy is primarily an essentially plural enterprise in which the many focus on the One in holiness and adoration, and that mutual focus draws them together. If the priest usurps the focus by becoming the actor, or the people become the focus for the priest who has nothing else to look at, the center of worship can literally displace God from the circle.

VP and EP simply represent two very different models, not just for the liturgy but for the church: one focused inward primarily on itself and its concerns, the other looking outward and onward; one emphasizing the gathering (with the clergy literally *against* the people) turned toward each other; the other the whole gathered body (with the clergy leading the people) turned toward the transcendent presence of God. What we have in these two models is, in short, the circle or the procession. Both have their place, but there is a question as to which better builds community. As mentioned above, there are situations in which the circular arrangement for the Eucharist makes good sense: a permanently or situationally closed community (a convent or school). But in these cases the strong sense of community already exists; in fact, the stronger this sort of community, the harder it is for an outsider to feel welcome—it is very hard to break into a circle, but it is wonderfully easy to slip in at the end of a procession.

Community is far more easily built by adding a sense of common direction and mission, rather than focusing on the membership itself. This is particularly true when the VP is circular in name only—for example, when a gothic church's high altar is moved forward by about a third or less, with the celebrant on one side and the congregation on the other. This has all of the weaknesses of both models, and I will reflect at greater length below on how this setup, far from creating an aura of equality, can be even more clericalizing in its effects than the most distant high altar of the old tradition.

Perhaps this is as good a place as any to mention the now relatively common practice of proclaiming the Gospel from the midst of the congregation—an innovation that came into fashion in the middle of the last century, and which, in many churches, means proclamation from some point in the center aisle, rather than from the other options offered first by the rubric: "from the same lectern [as the Lessons], or from the pulpit" (BCP 406). The intended symbolism is powerful; but the effect can be less so, as it may render the proclamation both invisible and inaudible except to those fortunate enough to be standing close to the center aisle. Proclamation from a more visible position would seem to preserve both the dignity of what is proclaimed, and the natural way of announcing good news directly to a gathering, slightly above and facing them, rather than from the middle of the crowd.

None of this is to say that the circular model for the ministry of word and/or sacrament can never work. I have seen and experienced worship in modern churches that embrace the circular model with success, usually constructed with this in mind: balancing the aspects of leadership of and membership in the body, without losing a sense of direction. For example, Saint Matthew and Saint Timothy's in Manhattan, redesigned and rebuilt after a disastrous fire, provides an intimate and almost womblike gathering place for the assembly (who enter via a long corridor that echoes the sacred caves and catacombs of antiquity). This church manages to preserve a marvelous sense of the transcendent, as the central altar is bathed in light from a clerestory atrium above, and the liturgical direction becomes *up*. The priest in this case is clearly leading the liturgy, but is also clearly a member of the circle, directing the attention of the whole assembly with word and gesture but also joining with them in raising their hearts on high together.

That sense of a community joined in a common direction is at the heart of the liturgy. In *The Four Loves*, C.S. Lewis describes the difference between friendship and erotic love in terms of such focus: that lovers look at each other, and friends stand side by side looking toward some common interest (61). Clearly, the church is called to be a loving community, but the church's love is based on the sense of God as the ultimate lover, toward whom all our attention ultimately turns, and from whom we gain our life and power to love others, most especially those not already part of our circle. If we become fixated on each other in the liturgical assembly, rather then turning our attention to God, where will we get the emotional and spiritual energy to carry our love for God out into the world, instead of spending it all on ourselves? I'm sure we have all experienced being a visitor in a church (and all churches seem to think they are "welcoming") only to find ourselves at the coffee hour after worship vainly trying to break into one of the circles of members who have time only to relate to folk they already know.

Furthermore, if the priest must become the "stand-in" for Christ, does that not place upon him or her an intolerable need both to "deliver" and to receive the displaced love of the whole congregation, rather than leading and guiding that love toward the transcendent One who is before us, beyond us, above us, and yet at the same time with us? Seeking to reveal Christ through one's own "gestures, prayer, and facial expressions" (as the Congregation on Divine Worship recommended) strikes me as the cult of the personality verging on idolatry: and any priests who succeeded in doing so would likely be a danger to their congregations and to themselves. I am reminded of a short story from Ray Bradbury's *The Martian Chronicles* in which a shape-shifting Martian becomes the object of the inmost need of each person he encounters (including a priest, who sees him as the crucified Christ). Ultimately the conflicting needs of the people destroy the poor empathetic alien. Is there any connection between placing the clergy in this sort of position and some of the cases of clerical misconduct and burnout that seem to have become so common? I wonder.

I am more secure in saying that the processional form for the liturgy provides a responsible and at the same time less debilitating model for leadership and mission. First of all, there is a clear sense of direction, implying motion, or at least an expectancy of motion, a sense of a yet-to-be-realized *eschaton*, reminding us that even our Eucharist is a type and shadow of the glory that shall be, and not its full accomplishment. Secondly, the goal and focus is not within the community, but beyond it. And thirdly, and perhaps most importantly, the priest is the leader but not the goal.

Finally, to mention the deacon again: how much more powerful is the dismissal of the assembly as a sending forth in a particular direction, rather than as the mere dispersal of a circle. I have more than once heard the traditional oblong church model dismissed as an "airplane." At least airplanes go somewhere.

SO WHERE DO WE GO FROM HERE?

I realize in all of this that I risk being catalogued as the worst kind of retrograde liturgical reactionary. And I admit that I am a bit uncomfortable to find that I share any opinion at all with Pope Benedict XVI (or his earlier self as Cardinal Ratzinger). I was amazed when his *Splendor of the Liturgy* appeared, decrying the great "mistakes" of Vatican II, in which I can only say I felt as if he'd been reading my mind, if not my journal notes.

But I am heartened to find that my thoughts on this matter were presaged by the likes of Bonnell Spencer and Josef Jungmann, and today are echoed by numerous younger clergy and laity. Moreover, my practical experience has also shown me that a balanced liturgy, with elements of the liturgy of the word (particularly the readings and the sermon) presented in an engaging, lively, and personable manner, coupled with a liturgy of the table that brings with it notes of transcendence, solemnity, and purpose, has provided the congregations where I have led, served, and worshiped with a real sense of renewal. Where some have abandoned the old "high altar" and introduced freestanding altars, it is possible to reverse the situation in favor of the manner of worship that has been predominant for most of Christian history—not because of the historical reality, but because people are hungry for transcendence in a world that so aggressively confronts them or performs for them, rather than accompanying them and leading them.

Simply rearranging the furniture is not an answer to church growth or mission in itself. Nor is simply changing the posture of the clergy in relation to the laity. What the church needs is a complete attitude adjustment and recovery of what it means to worship the One who is the object of our prayer, and the source of our life. Let us mean what we say, do what we intend, and become what we behold.

KNOWN IN BREAD

THE EUCHARIST AT THE HEART OF WORSHIP

> As they came near the village to which they were going, he walked ahead as if he were going on. But they urged him strongly, saying, "Stay with us, because it is almost evening and the day is now nearly over." So he went in to stay with them. When he was at the table with them, he took bread, blessed and broke it, and gave it to them. Then their eyes were opened, and they recognized him; and he vanished from their sight. (Luke 24:28–31)

It may be hard to believe, but every time we Christians gather to share in the Holy Eucharist we are surrounded by miracles and swept up into mysteries. Miracles need not be overtly supernatural so long as they produce faith. That is, the importance of miracles does not lie in whether they appear to defy the laws of science or reason, but in what they work upon the human spirit, leading us into all truth, revealing God's presence to the eye of faith, parting the curtain of the mystery for a moment to let the mortal behold and adore the immortal.

You may have heard of the miraculous tortillas that occasionally appear on the griddles of devout women in Mexico. Now, these tortillas do not miraculously appear as manna from heaven, discovered in the morning with the risen dew, already baked and ready for gathering, with a double portion on the eve of the Sabbath. No, the miracle about these tortillas lies in the fact that scorched into the surface of these otherwise quite ordinary flatbread pancakes is the appearance of the likeness of Christ. Perhaps you've seen photographs of these miraculous tortillas, literally turning up to confront, amaze, and delight Mexican housewives as they flip them over on the griddle. When such tortillas "turn up," they are dried and preserved in cigar boxes lined with colorful wrapping paper, adorned with plastic flowers, and reverently placed on shelves of the homes blessed with this miraculous visitation.

And of course this can produce two reactions in the blasé and sophisticated *norteamericano*. We might simply snigger and laugh up the sleeve at these quaint folk with their charming superstitions. Or we could take the cool approach of science and say that all of this has a simple and rational explanation: that the human brain, with its need and ability to read pattern into chaos, can see the likeness of Christ in the random scorches on the surface of the baked tortilla, much as one can look at clouds and see them forming ships at sea, castles in Spain, or an entire zoo of fluffy animals.

Yet even though the miraculous tortilla may have a fairly rational, simple explanation, and although we may be tempted to dismiss it as a superstitious triviality, that doesn't mean it isn't a miracle. For it *brings* faith and *nourishes* faith—and it is faith, not magic, that is truly miraculous. Faith is the reason miracles happen in the first place, whether the heart disposed toward God is open to accept the gift, or the soul turned away from God receives a gentle (or not so gentle) tap on the shoulder to recall the straying and jaded eye to the heart and source of reality.

For the real miracle isn't that the face of Christ should appear on a tortilla; the real miracle—and this is the tap on the shoulder to us in the sophisticated third of the world—is that anyone should believe in a God who would be *interested* in having his face appear on a tortilla. The real miracle is to believe that God might be interested in surprising and blessing a poor Mexican housewife while she labors over a hot griddle at the end of a long day. The real miracle is to believe that God would be at all concerned with being in our midst—or any midst—today or any day, as we undertake our ritual acts of thanksgiving and prayer, rituals with their branches in the High Middle Ages and roots in the depths of the human psyche where the Awesome—what Otto called the *mysterium tremendum et fascinans*—lurks to raise the hairs on the backs of our necks. The real miracle is to believe that God would be interested in the wanderings of an insignificant tribe of desert nomads, little more than runaway slaves, and concerned enough to feed them for a generation on bread they had no better name for than "What *is* this?"; that the creator and governor of the universe could be at all concerned about the political affairs of a shepherd-boy turned-king; that the lord and maker of the vast expanse of interstellar space, of all time and matter and energy, could take the time and expend the energy to visit a young woman at her prayers and choose her to be the mother of the incarnate Son; and then choose to have her bear him in a barn; that God would, in that Son, live and die as one of us, and be raised from the dead, and then—the miracles continue—not immediately ascend to heaven, but continue those prosaic little field trips, having breakfast by the seaside, taking a walk with two disciples, breaking bread with them and then vanishing in a flash.

These are the miracles that surround us as we worship. It is a miracle that the bread of Emmaus and the manna of the wilderness are no more nor less a revelation of the presence of God than the scorched tortilla of Guadalajara, or the spotless host of Saint Swithin's by the Swamp. For it *is* in the simple actuality of bread, an everyday kitchen table commonplace, that *God has* chosen and *still* chooses to *be made known*—and *that* is a miracle if ever there was one!

And yet . . . and yet how slow humanity is to realize the miracle as it happens. Humankind looks for the technicolor, hi-res special effects of the apocalypse, while God stands revealed in the simple white-bread world around us. How slow of heart, like the children of Israel who looked at the manna with a shrug, and soon kvetched that it wasn't adequate food; how like the disciples who walked that road with Jesus, how slow to believe we are when we miss the presence of God with us, feeding us, walking at our side and opening the scripture to us, and breaking bread with us—the risen Lord who deigns to be our guest, the God who calls us no longer servants, but friends.

Jesus says (to them and to us), "How dull you are! How slow to believe the prophets!" And with this simple exclamation echoes God's never-failing amazement with Israel and with us. "When will you get it?" God seems to say. "How many seas must be parted, how many pillars of fire, how much deliverance, how much bread from heaven, how many crucifixions, how many risings from the dead until you understand *how much I love you?*"

God is ever-patient, but often speaks to people in this way. Just as Jesus walked with the disciples on that rural roadway, so God accompanied the children of Israel in their wandering in the wilderness, and brooded in their midst in the temple all those years. The prophets, from Moses to Mary Magdalene, have been discounted, ridiculed, and disbelieved by the very people who most needed to hear the news they bore. The church still stands divided, suffering with self-inflicted wounds while a world to which it was meant to bring good news looks on bemused.

Yet God does not abandon these stubborn children. God loves them—loves us—too much for that. And *that* is the greatest miracle, the greatest *faith*: *God's* faith in the children of God, in spite of their misbehavior; God's faith in the *friends* of God, in spite of their abandonment and scattering; God's faith in *us*. It is *that* faith, *God's faith in us*, to which God bids us open our eyes. God *does* not and *will* not leave us comfortless. The heart of our Christian faith is, as Evelyn Underhill put it, "not the memorial of a Death but the recognition of a continuing Life" (152). There is always time for another message, even a message from the Son of God, risen from the dead and alive forever. There is always more abundant bread to be handed round, even though we thought that there were only five paltry loaves.

God's faith in us is such that even when we doubt and disbelieve, God stoops to make us aware of the Real Presence with us, coming into our midst in a miracle that startles us by its simplicity, that shames us by its audacious condescension. God comes to us in *bread*, in *daily bread*. God startles us with the miracle of turning up on a tortilla. God challenges us with this notion: that the infinite expanse of God's being—compared to which all creation is as small as a hazelnut, as small as a spear-wound—that the vastness of divinity can be made so small that the gate of heaven opened by this saving victim turns out to be no wider than what can be held in the fingers'-breadth width in the center of a paten or—wonder of wonders—held in the palm of one's hand; that the God who created the universe should be made known in bread.

Baruch atah Adonai Elohenu, Melek ha'olam, ha'motzi lechem min ha'aretz. Blessed are you, Lord our God, everlasting King, the bringer-forth of bread from the earth. *Adesto! Adesto! bone pontifex, in medio nostri, sicut fuisti in medio discipulorum tuorum.* Be present, be present, O Good High Priest, in our midst as you were in the midst of your disciples. O come, let us worship, alleluia.

Evelyn Underhill

10

THE DAY THOU GIVEST

THE DAILY OFFICE AS COSMIC DANCE

> The heavens declare the glory of God, *
> and the firmament shows his handiwork.
> One day tells its tale to another, *
> and one night imparts knowledge to another.
> Although they have no words or language, *
> and their voices are not heard,
> Their sound has gone out into all lands, *
> and their message to the ends of the world.
> In the deep has he set a pavilion for the sun; *
> it comes forth like a bridegroom out of his chamber;
> it rejoices like a champion to run its course.
> It goes forth from the uttermost edge of the heavens
> and runs about to the end of it again; *
> nothing is hidden from its burning heat. (Psalm 19, BCP)

The nineteenth psalm begins with a wonderful, cosmic image of the heavens declaring God's glory as they slowly revolve, one day telling its tale to another, one night imparting knowledge to another, a kind of cosmic Algonquin Round Table of the stars, the sun, and the moon, who tell and retell God's glory even though they do not have words or language, and their voices are not heard.

Modern science, of course, thanks to Copernicus and Galileo, reverses the image. It isn't the heavens that spin about a stable earth, but a spinning earth whose rotation is but one of many complex movements in a vast celestial engine, something once captured in interlocking brass, now portrayed through computer graphics. Our imagery has changed, for as charming (or alarming) as the image may be, the sun is not actually let out of his bridegroom's chamber to run from one end of the world to the other. No, the sun is relatively immobile; it is the earth that slowly and majestically turns to sun itself evenly on all sides, turning and turning as it rotates day by day. From a vantage point far enough away in space, perpendicular to a line drawn from the sun to the earth, one could watch the shadow of night pass into the break of day from east to west, as a long band of dawn transects the earth from north to south. This moving band of transitional light is known to science by the ominous name "the terminator"—but one might just as well call it "the instigator"; for as night ends, day begins, and though from a terrestrial vantage point the sun goes down (or appears to go down), as the Preacher and Hemingway after him observed, the sun also rises.

To return to the scientists, the late physicist Richard Feynman, known for his quirky and offbeat genius, observed in a 1973 Yorkshire Television interview that wherever that terminator, that band of dawn, passes over an area populated by human beings, there exists, simultaneously with it, a band of people stretching from north to south and moving like a giant stadium wave from east to west—all brushing their teeth. And this great wave of terminator tooth-brushing sweeps across and around the globe as surely and substantially as the band of dawn itself, leaving behind the faint odor of mint.

But you and I know there is another diurnal and nocturnal cycle at work in the world. You and I know there is something else that happens as the dawn moves across the world, and as noonday, and evening, and night do the same. There is something else that sweeps around the globe besides sunlight and peppermint. Some of us remember the days when not just four but eight successive bands moved around the world like this. Matins, lauds, prime, tierce, sext, nones, vespers, and compline skimmed across the surface of the earth by day and by night, coating it with prayer. So it is that the bands move in their ordered rounds, and you can hear them singing, telling and retelling God's glory in many languages, day and night imparting knowledge to each other, as their voice goes out unto all lands.

The church's life of ordered prayer has a deep and intimate involvement with the cosmos. Even though we know that all times are in God's hand, and that one day or one hour isn't really more important than another in God's eyes, still we echo the cosmic rotations and revolutions of the earth and sun and moon in our prayers and our liturgy. It is no accident that the invention of timepieces in the Christian West owes its impetus to the need for the monks to keep their aptly named *hours*. And so they have kept them for centuries, mirroring the cosmos in miniature, like the precious illuminations in a book of hours, *telling* the hours, the days, the seasons, and the years of our Lord.

Apart from the grand cycles such as the scary and nervous-making millennium, or the festive Jubilee year, and other such generational anniversaries, our stateliest liturgical pace takes its rhythm from the yearly cycle of the seasons, from Advent through Christmas, and on beyond that pivotal commemoration to Epiphanytide, the elastic time that stretches out toward or shrinks away from Lent depending on the date of Easter, that queen of feasts whose mobility is still determined by the moon, the inconstant moon, grown full upon the footsteps of the equinox, spring's equal balance of day and night; so linked are we still to the heavens' movements that even secular governments take their direction, at least to this extent, from the church's obedience to rules laid down for an ancient people's spring festival of their deliverance, in which the church now shares by grace. Then on we course again to bright red Pentecost and on through the greenery to Holy Cross, the year fully marked and quartered with stational ember days, and finally back to Advent once again, our year decked and draped with liturgically colored prayer all along the way.

Those who take part in the church's worship find their attention to all this focused by altar guilds and liturgical leaders—and catalogs from the providers of church furnishings. But surely as well we follow the course of readings in the lectionaries, and proclaim the Gospels and reflect on the texts that recite the round of the year from expectation through birth and baptism, on to death and resurrection. The whole church resonates like a huge bell to those words so closely bound up with those seasons—the seasonal prefaces that lead to the great hymn of praise the church raises as it joins with the angels who from their vantage look down upon our world as it processes round the sun: Holy, Holy, Holy Lord, God of power and might, heaven and earth really are full of your glory.

On a smaller scale there is the monthly cycle of the Psalter, perhaps Thomas Cranmer's simplest and most thoughtful gift to those who follow the measured rule of its recitation. The Daily Office Lectionary of the 1979 Book of Common Prayer provides a seven-week cycle for reading the psalms, but Cranmer's old thirty-day rotation is still tucked in the headings scattered through the Psalter, and some prefer this monthly ordered reading, rather than the somewhat jerky and page-flippant version of the seven-week cycle. Perhaps more importantly, Cranmer's manner of recitation includes the whole thing, and retains all the bits of psalmody the other renders optional or omits entirely. Following his lead allows the reader to fulfill John Cassian's advice to internalize all of the emotions of the Psalter: "When we sing the Psalms, we remember all that our carelessness has brought on us, or our effort has secured, or divine providence has granted to us, or slippery and subtle forgetfulness lost to us, or human weakness brought about in us" (*Dialogues* IX, 18).

William White, our first presiding bishop, was no fan of Cranmer's monthly cycle, in part because he thought it improper for people to recite *all* of the Psalms, thereby putting into their mouths peculiar emotions that they did not feel. A good rational Enlightenment concern, no doubt, but perhaps not so wise concerning human nature after all. It is, in this as in so much else about worship, good to be reminded that "it's not about me"—but *us*, the big Us of the whole church and beyond it, sharing a common humanity prone to many failings. When those troubling passages of cursing and incrimination appear on our lips in this ordered recitation, it is therapeutic to be reminded we had best not place ourselves in the position of the righteous doing the cursing, but imagine ourselves as the *object* of those curses—that our own consciousness be purged and washed clean. We gain something in this ordered and full reading—in addition to facing those hard nuggets of frail or vicious human reality that make the psalms a challenge.

And perhaps we may equally relish the sometimes dissonant intersections of joyous feasts with penitential psalms—much as one can enjoy the dissonances of passing notes yearning for resolution in a Bach chorale, or the sharp bite of a peppercorn in an otherwise mild sauce. The hard bits and the dissonances we encounter in this orderly reading—as we do in the reality of life itself—both serve as reminders that on the heavenly scale, the orderly laws of gravitation and of physics, as they

King David presents the Psalter to Saint Benedict of Nursia

work upon the substance of the cosmos, will sometimes have the effect of wiping out the dinosaurs.

Then there is our weekly cycle, centered on Sunday, but inherited from a deeper and far older tradition that deliberately mirrored step-by-step the act of creation itself, and stubbornly stuck to it for all these years in spite of the fact that 7 doesn't go into either 30 or 12 or 365. This is another of those things in which the world joins the church in a life that revolves around Sunday—one thing upon which sacred and secular are of a common mind (with no offense to the dowager duchess of *Downton Abbey*, who apparently had never heard of a "weekend"). So powerful is the ancient memory of God's creative act that only the French were bold enough, during their Revolution, to attempt to metricize the week. It didn't last, and the primacy of seven regained its place.

And finally, we return to where we started, the smallest and the fastest spinning wheel in this great cosmic mechanism: the day God gives us day by day, and which we bless and sanctify with prayer, with daily breaking of the daily bread, and most especially with the Daily Office. In recognition of the role we play in the divine cosmic dance, the Daily Office has, since at least the time of Benedict himself, been called by that astounding and awe-inspiring name: the Work of God.

Now, in spite of its antiquity and universality, the Daily Office is one of those things that some people, even in the church, just don't get. I recall something that a secular priest said to me some years ago. I use the paradoxical phrase "a secular priest" because that's exactly what he was—a priest with no connection to a religious community. Well, this priest had just attended a life profession liturgy for one of my brothers in the Brotherhood of Saint Gregory. This profession of vows took place in the context of a celebration of the Holy Eucharist, which was set on a Saturday afternoon to allow for friends and family to attend. The liturgy ran late into the day, as such liturgies do, and afterward the assembly repaired to the refectory for a meal. After about forty minutes, it was time for Evening Prayer, and the brothers began to excuse themselves to return to the chapel. I happened to be sitting across the table from the secular priest, who asked where we were going. When I told him that it was time for Evening Prayer, he looked at me with astonished disbelief and said, with a somewhat scornful tone, "You're going to pray *again*!?" I looked at him, probably a bit surprised, and simply said, "Why, yes; it's what we *do*."

I'm afraid he didn't grasp the point, as many, sadly even in the church, don't. The irony is that the "secular" are not truly *worldly* in the sense of being as deeply in touch with the movements of the cosmos as the "religious," whose life of ordered prayer reflects that cosmos in miniature. The "secular" have followed the course that Richard Baxter described, so caught up with scholarship, didacticism, or activism that they have lost the simple gift of contemplation. Prayer, especially formal prayer, has been minimized or postponed or deferred almost out of existence, evaporated in a cloud of unfulfilled "intentions" as these busy workers imagine themselves to be getting about the *real* work of the church, the *real* work of God, the real *mission* of the church, as they see it.

But in so doing, they have seriously gotten hold of the wrong end of the stick. As Kenneth Leech wrote some years ago, far too many clergy are spending too much time in the wrong kind of office. It is good to recall that the Catechism in the Book of Common Prayer (855) begins its response to the question, "How does the Church pursue its mission?" by stating, "The Church pursues its mission as it prays and worships. . . ." The ordered prayer of the church is a large part of what the church is; it *is* the work of the church as much as it is the work of God, the church's mission and God's mission: "to restore all people to unity with God and each other in Christ." It is what the church is *for*.

And I mean the *whole* church. For I do not embrace the idea that the religious sisters and brothers, or even the clergy, are simply the professionals who pray for those who don't have the time—in spite of the fact that they sometimes end up doing so; and thank God someone does. We have it on good authority that ten righteous ones could once have saved a city from annihilation; and the rabbis still speak of God's preservation of the whole world on account of the fifty souls whose prayers forfend its utter collapse into nothingness. So yes, the good sisters and brothers and clerics *do* pray for others, but not so that those others can be let off the hook of praying for themselves. It is rather because this is a particular "vocation"—"work" *of* God, *for* God, and *from* God. This work of prayer may indeed help to hold the prayer-free and carefree world together, as the monks and nuns, the sisters and brothers—together with all the clergy and laity who preserve the practice of this *opus Dei*, this work of God in the Daily Office—lay down those daily fresh coats of prayer upon a spinning world. This vicarious benefit to the prayer-free *may* be one of the *effects* of this round of ordered prayer, but I want to be quite clear that it is not its primary raison d'être. If I can use the analogy of the theology of marriage, this is a *good* of daily prayer, but it is not its *end*. Its end is, as I wrote in an earlier chapter, in large part to call together the community of the faithful, to *make* the church as its scattered members are recalled to unity in Christ.

So while it is true that some do pray for others, passing the sandbags down the line to stay the flood, this is not the ideal for the church. On the contrary, one could wish that all of God's people were, if not prophets, at least committed to some form of daily prayer, even if it only took the form of one short office a day, a quickly uttered Lord's Prayer on arising, or even a wordless pause to summon to mind the name of God, invoking and re-membering God in that instant invocation. This is the vision that Saint Francis held when he conceived the idea of the Third Order: that even those living "in the world" could be religious through the devotion of their hearts toward God, consecrated with a rule that called upon them to praise and pray to God day and night, with the Lord's Prayer on their lips.

As for the clergy, I espouse that rather old-fashioned idea that Kenneth Leech was defending (and which is still on the books in the Church of England, though much ignored): that all clergy, secular and regular alike, should follow the daily discipline of ordered prayer laid down in the Daily Office. Thus joined with the laity, the varied orders of the whole church can exercise their responsibility and take up their share of the work of God, the *church's* work of God.

For the ordered life of daily prayer is the heart and soul of the work of God, of our work, our *liturgy* that is both the work for and of the people, and the work of God: for without God inspiring the will and the deed, without God's Holy Spirit filling and lifting our sails, our poor small boats would not be able to navigate the waters of creation.

God's Spirit hovered over those waters at the beginning, setting up the ripples that would become time and space and all that is. Our ordered life of prayer reflects the movements of the cosmos, one voice taking up the song as another dies out, as those bands of dawn and dusk and midday and midnight sweep around the earth. But the daily work of prayer does not only reflect the rolling cycles of the cosmos. There is a greater mystery still: that the work of prayer *reinforces* those ripples of the Spirit to such an extent that it helps birth the universe into more than it was before we prayed. As Marjorie Hewitt Suchocki has said so eloquently, "God works with the world as it is in order to bring it to where it can be. Prayer opens the world to its own transformation" (19). And that includes us. Our prayer will one day reach to the edges of the created universe. The vision of the psalmist was of mountains skipping like rams, and hills like young sheep, of the sun and moon and stars telling of the glory of God, and of every creature with breath in its mouth raising its voice to praise the Lord. And we are, *pace* Galileo and Copernicus, at the middle of it all, we on this blue marble on which God chose to be incarnate, scandalously particular in our smallness, lowly handmaids graced by that visitation and exalted from our humble place on the outer arm of the Milky Way, and given an awesome task. This is the work of God, God's work in us and our work for God with God's people.

As John Ellerton wrote:

We thank thee that thy Church, unsleeping
while earth rolls onward into light,
through all the world her watch is keeping
and rests not now by day or night.
As o'er each continent and island
the dawn leads on another day,
the voice of prayer is never silent,
nor dies the strain of praise away. (Hymnal 1982, 24)

This prayer, this daily prayer, ordered and repeating and mirroring the rhythms of God's good world, of God's great universe, is the work of God and our work too. It's what we do.

WHY WE PRAY

PRAYER AS PRAXIS, PRAXIS AS PRAYER

> Our beseeching is not the cause of God's goodness. . . . This he showed in truth when he said all these sweet words, "I am the ground of your beseeching. . . ." Our Lord himself is the first receiver of our prayer, in my view, and takes it most thankfully, rejoicing greatly in it; he sends it up above and sets it in his treasury, where it shall never perish. It is there, before God with all his saints, continually being received and continually responsive to our needs. (Julian 41)

Why do we pray? Specifically, Why do we pray *for* things? Such a question must seem an odd island discovered at this point in this sea of reflections. It might seem less strange, coming almost as an accusation, from an atheist who saw prayer simply as a waste of time and energy, a futile chase after the wind, shouting down the empty hallways of forlorn and meaningless hopes, love letters addressed to a vacant building or calls made to a disconnected telephone.

But even those who do pray, those who sometimes hope against hope, who love when love seems not to be returned, who persist in lighting candles instead of cursing the darkness, who continue to send out the SOS even when the airwaves are silent and no response appears to be forthcoming—even those who do continue to pray are often moved, in a dark night of doubt, to ask the same question, "Why *am* I doing this?"

Julian of Norwich herself, a woman so imbued with the spirit of prayer that she must have glowed in the dark, could say, "Oftentimes our trust is not full, for we are not secure that God hears us as we think, for our unworthiness and lack of feeling; because we are often as barren and dry after praying as we were before." And she adds the touching confession, "So have I myself felt" (41). If such a one as Julian can admit to spiritual dryness, how much more can we?

This collection of essays is cast as navigation in the ocean of liturgical theology. I frame this exploration here as seeking an answer to the question—Why do we pray?—prompted by the liturgical evidence before us.

Some people doubt the existence of God; some people who acknowledge the possibility or the reality of God may still doubt the utility or efficacy of prayer. And sometimes even people who pray—even masters of contemplative prayer like Julian of Norwich, and masters of active praxis like Teresa of Calcutta—will find themselves becalmed in the sea of despondency, doubtful of the use of prayer, perhaps even doubtful of the existence of God. But when all is said and done, whatever the doubts about the existence of God or the usefulness of prayer, *no one doubts the existence of prayer*. When asked, "Do you believe in infant baptism?" a bishop once replied, "Believe in it? Why, man, I've *seen* it!" This is the fact before us: prayer exists. And from this datum we can furthermore derive a maxim, *orare humanum est*: to pray is human. People pray, even sometimes when it seems the most illogical, impractical thing in the world. People pray. Even those who ridicule it or find it utterly meaningless cannot deny that prayer is and always has been a part of the human character. As the old saying borne of the experience of warfare has it, there are no atheists in foxholes. People pray.

Prayer is, then, an almost universal human experience, from the dawn of human consciousness—the awareness of self that implies the awareness of The Other. Among the first responses to the primitive intimation of Rudolf Otto's *mysterium tremendum*—the sense that we are in the presence of something other and greater than ourselves—is the impulse to *pray* to that other and greater. And I believe that the existence of prayer points us not only to the actuality of God, but tells us something about the *nature* of God, something perhaps truer and more dynamic and more lovely and lively than we have been taught to expect by systematic theologians.

The great medieval systematizers of the Christian faith, those scholastic theologians, the sententious and scholastic quibblers and questioners, often took Aristotle for their model instead of Abraham. They often focused on study rather than worship, and their questions and conclusions therefore resound more with the echoes of the debating hall than with those of the sanctuary. Even if they were not literally concerned with the number of angels dancing on a pinhead, they were certainly blissfully unconcerned to know if in fact the angels danced. So they often deduced (or reduced) God in the image of essential being more than of dynamic loving. And they posited many things about God, carefully argued to be sure, though often a bit shaky when followed back to the assumptions that underlay the propositions.

The view that the scholastic academy adopted has customarily come to be called the "Greek" way of doing theology. This does scant justice to the patristic theologians of the East and West, who focused less on the existence of God than on the nature of God, but we can use the term with that caveat in mind. The "Greek" theologians (many of whom were actually Latin) so focused on matters of essence and substance that to a large extent they lost sight of the complementaries to their doctrines, the corrective exceptions to their ordered rules, which they thought they had fenced and parried aside with so many *sed contras*, some of them resting on the thinnest ground of proof text. They forgot that you cannot capture flame in a bottle, least of all the flame of God's Holy Spirit. Most importantly, in their efforts to develop a rigidly systematic theology, they came to use scripture primarily as a source for isolated texts to make a point or parry an objection, but sometimes missed the broader concepts portrayed not at the level of phrase or verse, but at the level of saving story.

More than that, the "Greek" theologians too often divorced liturgical and spiritual reality from their consideration (or undertook a trial separation). In doing so, they walled off the experience of the faithful with it, and lost sight of the deep truth that while we cannot completely define the incomprehensible God, the faithful can and do gesture in the general direction that faith and hope assure us is Godward.

That gesture is the substance of worship and of prayer, the literal embodiment of human hopes—the outstretched, upraised hand that wards away judgment, or beseeches a boon or a blessing, or offers the prayer of praise and thanksgiving. We have not got God figured out. God remains mysterious and tremendous, and it is no accident, given our startling confrontation with the divine, that the position adopted by the leader of prayer, the posture we call *orans,* bears resemblance to a holdup, and that among the first things God's messengers to mortals have to say is, "Do not be afraid." The posture of prayer and worship is one of astonishment and humility, whether we raise our hands or fall to our knees. For in those moments we are in the presence of the truly and ultimately astonishing and absolutely humbling. The reality of prayer assures us not merely that God *is,* but that God is to be worshiped and adored.

As God told Moses from the burning bush, "This shall be the *sign* for you that it is I who sent you: when you have brought the people out of Egypt, you shall *worship* God on this mountain" (Exod. 3:12). That is, the evidence, the sign, the proof that God is Who God claims to Be, will be found in the fact and act of worship. It is not too bold, then, to add one more proof of God to the theological arsenal of scholastic arguments—ontological, teleological, moral, and so on—the *liturgical* argument: we may well worship *what* we do not know, but we do well know *that* we worship.

The Quality of Mercy and All Else

The scholastic theologians working in the "Greek" style were interested in first causes, given their goal of philosophical exposition (regardless of the patristic warning about a wall of separation between Athens and Jerusalem). They chart for us a God who is infinite, omniscient, omnipotent, and impassible. And let me hasten to add, before I am accused of rash heresy, that there is a truth in each of these epithets. But they are not by any means the end of the story, and taken by themselves, as they usually are in the scholastic catalog of God's attributes, they are not even the beginning, for they do not take fully into account the evidence of scripture in its fullness (as God speaking to the human heart through human hearts) or the actuality of prayer (the human heart speaking to the heart of God).

For if God is *only and utterly* infinite, omniscient, omnipotent, and impassible, what is the use of prayer to such a God? I mean that question in all of its ambiguity and ambivalence: what use to us, *or* to God? What use at all?

Why pour out our needs and hopes to a God who already knows all that is and will be, who can do everything, but cannot move or be moved to do anything: a God who strictly speaking cannot have unmet desires and is impassible to human hopes? The theologians—although they were anticipated by the prophets long before—were right to move us away from a God who craves the smell of burning livestock and appears to be capable of being bought off if sufficient quantities of cattle meet a bloody and fiery end. But they went too far in the other direction, in their urge to keep God detached from the world, to the point that God could have no conceivable interest *in* the world. Simply speaking, in the categories of such theologians, prayer to a God who is utterly impassible is—subjectively and objectively—ultimately no different from prayer to a God who doesn't exist at all. The savage God of the sacrificial altar might as well be tamed into what someone once called "a nice old man who likes to be read to" but who doesn't understand a word we're saying.

Yet still the old, old story continues to be told and told again, as the scrolls are unrolled year by year, as the page-edges of the pocket Testaments darken and lose their gilding to the human sweat of anxious searching for comfort and assurance. Yet still the church her watch is keeping; still her prayer goes on. The smoke continues rising from the altar, though now compacted of the bloodless sacrifice of incense, which signifies the prayers of the saints, and from the prayers themselves. And so it goes, I firmly believe, not simply because God *is* but because God *loves*, because God *is love*. The scholastics, in their wish to preserve God's monarchy, impassibility, and uniform simplicity, neglected and downplayed (even if they did not entirely forget) the rich dynamism of the Trinity and the radical implications of the Incarnation—a dynamism and connectedness witnessed to in the irreducible fact of prayer.

The theologians were so afraid to place limits on God that they forgot the fruits of Julian's first vision: that even within the limits of a circle there are infinitely many points; that even in—and for us mortals *only in*—the finite Jesus Christ can the infinite Trinity be understood at all (4). They forgot that, as Julian saw so clearly, "the supreme point that may be seen in Christ's passion is to think and know what he *is* who suffered. . . . Who as long as he was passible suffered and sorrowed for us; but now that he is risen and no more passible, yet he suffers with us" (20).

They neglected (mostly in the West, obsessed as it was with sin) this astonishing implication of the Incarnation and its ability to communicate the idiomatic humanity of Jesus Christ into the eternal verity of the Godhead, where it, and we through it, together are wrapped and enclosed in God's embrace. They neglected that God's knowledge is not limited merely to *all that is*, but encompasses *all that can possibly be*, not just the present realities but all the infinite possibilities stretching out to the horizon of culmination where all will be well, and all will be well, and all manner of thing will be well.

They neglected that God is the ground not simply of being but of becoming, as God's creatures act and react in response to the love that moves them, a love that comes from God and returns to God through the mystery of the Incarnate Christ. They forgot that God's temporal activity cannot be separated from, nor subsist apart from, God's eternal Sabbath rest, in a great both/and that Christ affirmed when he said his Father has never ceased working (John 5:17).

Julian understood that while God in Christ is glorious and impassible as our head, "yet concerning his body in which all his members are knit, he is not yet fully glorified or all impassible" (31). And it is this body, this body of Christ of which we are members, this body which is also his bride, the church that longs with the inward-groaning Spirit of God that cries out to God the Father, the church that thus experiences the Trinity in Unity: it is the church who tells its story and it is the church who prays. And the prayer itself—even the prayer of need and petition—comes to be because God, who is the ground of prayer as well as being, ordains it as a gift to the church, which the church in return presents to God, Christ's body enacting the sign of Christ's real presence, the sign of God's *isness*: *"and you shall worship."* And how the angels dance!

It is hard to imagine that Hasidic master Rabbi Nachman of Breslov had any familiarity with the Christian mystics. Yet because he was a man of deep and intense prayer, a man on fire with the love of God, I am firmly convinced that in the grace of God's dispensation for the Chosen people, and in the rabbi's fervent love and longing for the Messiah, he apprehended the same truths as Julian and other Christian mystics, transmuted in the language of his tradition. I must believe this as a corollary to the proposition of faith that God is One, and that those who have experienced the knowledge and love of God have shared in that knowledge and that love. I want to share with you a short parable Rabbi Nachman told, which strongly echoes the divine interplay of prayer that Julian describes. I first became acquainted with this story when I was working in the theater, for strange as it may seem I did more than my share of work in traditional and modern Yiddish theater. This version of Reb Nachman's tale appears in S. Ansky's mystical romance, *The Dybbuk*, a 1916 play in which, by the way, love conquers both death and theology. This is my version of the story, with some added detail from the early nineteenth-century original as Reb Nachman told it.

> At the farthest end of the world there stands a high mountain; and on top of the mountain there rests a huge rock; and from the rock there flows a clear spring of water. All the way at the other end of the world you can find the heart of the world—you know of course that everything has a heart and the whole world has one great heart, so great that the least part of it is greater than anything else. The heart of the world never takes its eye off the clear spring of water, but looks at it with deepest desire—pining and thirsting for the spring and its clear water—but the heart cannot take even one tiny step in its direction, because the moment the heart moves

from where it is by even a single step, it risks losing sight of the mountain crest and the rock and the spring; and if the heart were ever to lose sight of the spring, even for a fraction of a second, it would lose its life—and if the heart of the world were to perish, the whole world would die. So it longs and looks always toward the clear spring.

The clear spring has no experience of time; it is not within time. So how can it exist, you ask? It is given a day at a time, as a gift from the heart of the world. This gift sustains the spring day by day, but one day at a time is all that the heart gives it. When that day begins to come to a close, the spring starts to sing to the heart of the world, and the heart of the world joins it in song, singing to the clear spring. This song that the heart and the spring sing together spreads through the whole world, and threads of light emerge from the song, and the threads touch and enter the hearts of all things in the world—you recall I said that all things have a heart—and the threads flow to each heart and from one heart to another.

And there is a righteous man of grace who has an eye on all of this, one who collects all generous and good things of this world. And he gathers these threads of light coming from every heart of each thing—and he weaves them into time, enough time for just one day. And just as the old day is dying—and if it were to die the world would end, heaven forbid—at that very moment the man of grace arrives with the one day he has woven from the threads of light, and he gives it to the heart of the world. And it is this one day—this very one—that the heart of the world presents to the clear spring. And so it is that the clear spring lives another day.

I think you can see how this translates into language that Julian would have been at home with, especially if you see the man of righteousness and grace as the Incarnate and Anointed One. And it helps to lead me finally to provide an answer to my question, Why do we pray?

Scripture attests that God "is not a man that he should change his mind" (Num. 23:19), and this was a favorite proof-text for the sententious theologians who wished to prove God's immutability thereby—though the verse comes from the mouth of Balaam, admittedly echoed later by Samuel (1 Sam. 15:29). But this notion is tempered by a goodly number of texts which equally well describe a much more dynamic God. To reconcile these, ultimately we might best picture God less as *unchanging* and more as *constant*: that is, always moving in the same direction, and with the same constant intent for good; sometimes in "mysterious ways" beyond our understanding in the performance of wonders, but moving nonetheless. As another old hymn, "Great Is Thy Faithfulness," puts it, there is no "shadow of turning" with God, no suggestion of deviation

Based on the Christ of Mount Sinai

or lack of resolve in a perfect Will, a perfect Love, only the irrepressible movement to-us-ward that is the substance of grace, divine desire rushing to embrace human hope turned Godward—desire like that of the generous father of the prodigal son, not standing on the porch waiting for the apology, but rushing headlong to meet the beloved on the way. Ezekiel's vision of God's chariot holds true: the cherubic wheels turn, but always move "straight ahead" (1:9–12).

This is paradoxical, of course, but we can take Jesus's teaching into account to shed some light. Even though Genesis tells us that God completed the creation and entered a Sabbath rest on the seventh day (2:3), as I noted above, Rabbi Jesus assured those who condemned him for working on the Sabbath, "My Father is still working, and I also am working" (John 5:17). So there is a sense in which God is both at rest and at work at the same time, until all time shall cease; or resting in eternity while working in temporality, or as the other rabbi told, weaving one day at a time and presenting it as a gift to the world.

It is worth quoting another source, the recently rehabilitated Galileo. When the church insisted he declare the earth to be the immovable center of the universe (a cosmology derived in large part from that very theology of stasis and immutability the church's hierarchs had inherited from earlier times, buoyed by misapplied proof-texts), the old man, after agreeing with the official party line that the earth was stationary, is purported to have muttered under his breath, "And yet, it moves." And he was right, and the church was wrong.

Far be it from me to say that the church or its theologians are wrong about the nature of God. But just as the worldview that held the earth to be a stable and immovable center—quite logical when you consider that's what it seems to be as we watch the flighty sun rise and set, the inconstant moon wax and wane—just as this worldview made it so difficult to grasp the complexities of the cosmos as it actually is, so too what the church conceived aright about God has sometimes obscured or unbalanced other equally important truths.

Even some of the most fiercely academic theologians, Thomas Aquinas among them (about whom more to follow), did manage to catch glimpses of these neglected aspects of God amidst their questions and propositions. But it was the full-time mystics of the church, like Julian of Norwich, who came closer to the heart of God's incomprehensible nature, for they began their quest not with the academic notion of the pure Being of an impassible God, but with the liturgical actions of prayer, and most especially with the contemplation of Christ—and him in his passion. And while Julian was always at pains to defend the church's prerogative to teach all things rightly, she felt that tension between official teaching and her own apprehension of God, and lived in the richness of that dissonance, that passing tone in the chorale of her blessed life, seeking and finding resolution not in understanding, but in love: "Love was his meaning" (86).

The truth that Julian grasped is this: that our prayer is a gift to God made possible by God, which God does not need but which God uses to our good; that the heart of God is all movement even though at rest, all delight even though in pain, all charity and forgiveness even though rejected and crucified. She saw that above all in the Incarnation, God was pleased to dwell *within* our passible sensuality and bind it to the eternal divine image residing in our substance. Julian said:

> I saw that our humankind is in God whole . . . for the higher part of our nature is knit to God in creation, and God is knit to the lower part of our nature in taking our flesh. And thus in the person of Christ our two natures are at-oned. (57)

And this at-one-ment is the locus for prayer. Just as God will one day be our eternal home, so in the meantime God deigns to be our guest, and be at home with us, gracing the tables of our lives. What this means is that God is in an intimate and loving relationship with us, and this relationship tempers and shapes God's *immutability* to be an immutability of *intent*, an unshakable and self-giving *will* for the good of the other—which is about as fine a definition of love as you will find.

And God's *omniscience* is the knowledge not only of what will be, but of all possible being and doing, in which we too have our part to play as responsive contributors to God's working in the world, at work with our work of prayer—weaving our daily prayer into the gift of the time we use to pray, which is the Work of God. And God takes advantage of our contribution to bring about the best end for the world at every instant, gently guiding it with that constant and immutable love toward the day when all manner of thing will be well.

Our prayer, then, is not a bothersome pecking-away at God to get God's attention. Our prayer is not a therapeutic talking to ourselves to make ourselves feel better. Our prayer is nothing less than the hopeful gift we make of ourselves—our souls and bodies, reasonable and holy—to God, something God desires to receive, yet something God has given us to give. Prayer is the gift that opens us to transformation and gives God the joy of wooing the world into being moment by moment, day by day, and year by year, steadfast and unchanging in purpose, love, and grace.

Our prayer is a participation in God's creative and redemptive act, a creation and redemption that is once and for all and yet continuously unfolding day by day. At each moment God woos us forth to greet him, the Bridegroom, and accepts the gift of ourselves, the church as Bride, the one clothed in the white garments which are the righteous deeds of the saints (Rev. 19:8). Prayer is what we bring to this great occasion, to this great Bridegroom, this eternal Spouse: our prayer is our wedding gift to God.

Thomas Aquinas

The Knowledge and the Love of God

Limits of Our Quest, Extent of Our Song

> How unsearchable are [God's] judgments and how inscrutable his ways! "For who has known the mind of the Lord?" (Rom. 11:33–34)

Thomas Aquinas isn't what he used to be. In an era in which even Jesuits and Dominicans are adopting the insights of process theology, Thomism, that refined form of theological inquiry to which Aquinas gives his name, has slipped from the preeminent seat it once enjoyed. And if it hasn't completely buried them, the Vatican has at least cast a shroud of obscurity over those of Aquinas's teachings that it has ceased to find convenient.

No, Thomas simply isn't what he used to be. I am tempted to surmise that this little volume may be one of the few published this year in which the name of Thomas Aquinas is cited in more than just the footnotes. But I cite him in part because earlier in these essays I may have seemed to give systematic and scholastic theologians rather harsh treatment, and I would like to balance the picture a bit.

As you well know, Thomas Aquinas was a Dominican priest and theologian who applied his brilliance and skill to a massive work of systematic theology. Now, as you also know, a systematic theologian is not just someone who sketches out a few important articles, or writes a few books. These days it doesn't take much more than a contract with a publisher, a good agent, and a couple of talk-show appearances to end up being hailed as a theologian, or reviled as a heretic—especially if you're an Episcopal bishop. But in the old days, the road to being taken seriously as a systematic theologian was a long one, and the work that systematic theologians produced reflected that thoroughness and that depth. In the old days a systematic theologian would have felt it important to cover *all* the bases, from the soup of creation all the way through to the hard nuts of judgment.

And Thomas Aquinas very nearly did it, in the great *Summa Theologica*, which could loosely be translated as "Everything You Ever Wanted to Know About God and Just About Everything Else." For a man whose nickname was "The Dumb Ox," he had quite a bit to say. In thirty-eight treatises, thousands of articles, tens of thousands of responses and ripostes to every conceivable objection, Thomas Aquinas set out to systematize his search for God—and whether that search was a matter of faith seeking understanding or of understanding seeking faith is the matter before us.

The great work that Thomas undertook remains unfinished—not that he died before completing it. On the contrary, he stopped work on it by choice, at the very height of his productivity. His keen mind by that time had "justified God's ways to man" more than malt or Milton could either ever do. But he stopped, stopped within sight of the finish line.

For one day in early December 1273, Thomas was celebrating the Holy Eucharist. And in the midst of the liturgy, he stopped cold—or perhaps I should say, stopped warm. Something even he, with his remarkable ability to categorize and elucidate, couldn't describe—something happened to him in the midst of that sacrament's celebration, in the midst of that worship, in the midst of that liturgy, something happened that completely overpowered him. He caught a glimpse of the infinite

God he had tried so hard to pin down. And he decided never to write theology again.

His faithful secretary encouraged him to take up the work again, to bring his monumental system to completion. How much more might he perfect it in light of his recent experience? But Thomas replied, "I can do no more. Such things have been revealed to me that all I have written now seems to me to be like so much straw." Like his namesake, Thomas the Apostle, Thomas Aquinas saw something that made all of his questions fall apart, as he fell to his knees in adoration of his Lord and his God.

The one who had spent most of his life picking things apart, dividing them up into categories and organizing them into systems, confronted the One before whose utter unity and singularity all his pluriform complexity collapsed like a house of straw. The master of words fell silent before the supernal Word, with nothing left to say.

Paul wrote to the Romans, "O the depth of the riches and wisdom and knowledge of God! How unsearchable are his judgments and how inscrutable his ways! 'For who has known the mind of the Lord?'" (11:34). Thomas tried to know the mind of the Lord, and when the Lord deigned to appear to him that cold December morning, he realized he didn't know anything at all. Everything he thought he knew turned out to be so much mattress stuffing, the labor of his life turned flimsy and insubstantial in comparison with the solid and supersubstantial actuality that confronted him. How much all his learning now seemed to be like the offcast rubbish Saint Paul had once been so proud of, but had been willing to discard in light of the surpassing knowledge of God (Phil. 3:8).

But don't mourn for Thomas, any more than you would for Paul. On the contrary, rejoice; and again, I say, rejoice. In spite of the wistful tone one might read into his words to his secretary, Thomas appears not to have been unhappy about this development. On the contrary, he treasured it: for what he may have lost in realizing he had spent much of his life working at cross-purposes with God was incomparably compensated for by what he gained—for he gained what he'd really been after all the while. Because in addition to his effort to *know* God, Thomas had also devoted himself to an effort to *love* God.

This is why I want to be fair to the academic theologians; for most of them are people of profound faith and real piety, and not a few of them were (and a few still are) religious brothers or sisters living that ordered round of worship and prayer that has been so much the focus of my writing. While it is true that not a small number of theological scholars do manage to write and think their way out of the faith—or into a very different faith—as they spend more and more time in their studies and less and less in their stalls and sanctuaries, still there are those theologians who keep in touch with God through the time-tested disciplines of prayer and worship.

And Thomas was one of these. For in addition to the dense philosophical argumentation of his theological works, Thomas also wrote love songs to God. And while the pages of the *Summa* are rarely opened these days outside the walls of seminaries—if even there—the love songs Thomas wrote are still sung around the world. Five of them are in our current Episcopal hymnal.

Such hymns, great hymns set to great and timeless melodies, can capture our hearts and transport them in love. And the love songs that Thomas wrote capture as few other hymns do that poignant longing for the invisible, incomprehensible God who lies invitingly beyond our reach, beyond our grasp, outside our categories, transcending our systems.

We do not know what Thomas saw during the Holy Eucharist that December day, but I'd be willing to venture that God welcomed this faithful seeker more because of his love than his intellect, giving him a glimpse of the unseen verity he had so long humbly adored. Thomas the thinker could only see his own thoughts, the intellectual and analogical net he wove so fine that it obscured his vision, though it still couldn't catch the fish he was after. But Thomas the lover could see his beloved, however fleetingly, however briefly, and one look was enough to *do him in*. Not just the intellect, but its outer doorways—the senses of taste, touch, and vision—were overwhelmed by the outpoured Love of God, the doors of his mind creaked on their hinges, the veil was parted, and Thomas beheld that Love, however briefly, face-to-face, and was smitten to the soul by Love itself at first sight.

And so shall we be. We cannot all be systematic theologians—thanks be to God! But we can all *love* God, and we will find that love most fully expressed in our worship and liturgy, and in our active service to one another. When we do so, when we do what Thomas did that December day so long ago, we share in the holy mystery, this precious gift of the Holy Eucharist, in which our Lord and Savior Jesus Christ assures us that he is present, as he gives us his body and blood, this spiritual food and drink of new and unending life in him. Christ is truly present, and we behold our beloved.

Years ago, when I was in college in Baltimore, studying to be an actor, I was also active in the Episcopal Church—indeed I'd been so since rediscovering an adult faith in my first college year, thanks in no small part to the unlikely theological mixture of Alan Watts, C.S. Lewis, and Teilhard de Chardin. One of my best friends, a fellow actor in the theater company on campus, couldn't understand this. He was an agnostic, a slightly singed and somewhat bitter lapsed Roman Catholic who had survived the parochial school system as it was enforced in Baltimore in the days before Vatican II. My, did *he* have tales to tell. For myself, in spite of having been brought up "catholic," I'd escaped attending the parochial school system—and I've long thought that had I not gone to public school instead, I'd be a very unhappy Jesuit today.

But my friend, by this point, a few scant years after his liberation from the archdiocesan parochial school gulag, no longer believed in God—but he *did* believe in flying saucers. He had come to the belief that humanity was created and guided by space aliens, for some reason known only to them. He was always full of the latest news on sightings of spaceships, as proof of the existence of the aliens he believed in instead of God. (Ironically, his greatest fame as an actor came as a continuing character in several of the *Star Trek* sequels, and here am I, an Episcopal priest—who is to say our lives have, if not come to a logical conclusion, at least followed a logical course; that as Hamlet said, however much we may rough-hew them, there is after all a destiny that shapes our ends.)

Well, one day I told my friend I really didn't put much stock in the theory of aliens, though I was willing to look at the evidence. He responded,

"OK, then, when was the last time Jesus appeared?" Almost at once I said, "Last Sunday morning, on the altar at Trinity Episcopal Church!"

That is the truth, if we are prepared to accept it, as I think we are. Jesus comes to us today, and every day we gather at the table, hidden with, in, and under bread and wine, species far more truly and demonstrably present than any of an alien sort. In the Holy Eucharist we are granted a glimpse of Christ's presence, a glimpse granted to those who love him, to those who seek him, and who seeking, loving, find. In this we come to begin to know as we are known, for God also knows *us* not through intellect but through love, which is the very substance of God's being and doing. The knowledge and the love of God are one—both our knowledge and love directed Godward, and God's prevenient knowledge and love directed toward us, through the Incarnate Word who speaks in our hearts.

Saint Paul wrote to the Colossians: "I want their hearts to be encouraged and united in love, so that they may have all the riches of assured understanding and have the knowledge of God's mystery, that is, Christ himself, in whom are hidden all the treasures of wisdom and knowledge" (2:2–3).

These are the treasures, these the mysteries we have been seeking in these reflections. We have been on a quest, a sacred and holy quest for a goal beyond our limits. We cannot lay hold of the mystery here and now. We are to some extent like anglers who talk the most about the one that got away. We cannot know in this life as we are known, but we can—by grace—love as we are loved. In doing this we will find that the limit to our quest is not so far away after all. God may be beyond our grasp, but we are not beyond God's reach.

I will end this reflection with the words of Thomas Aquinas, the words of one of his love songs to God, written about eight years before his life-changing experience of 1273. The song ends like this:

> Jesus, whom now hidden, I by faith behold,
> what my soul doth long for, that thy word foretold:
> face to face thy splendor, I at last shall see,
> in the glorious vision, blessed Lord, of thee.

13

Teach Us to Pray

The Lord's Prayer as Microcosmic Re-creation

> He was praying in a certain place, and after he had finished, one of his disciples said to him, "Lord, teach us to pray, as John taught his disciples." (Luke 11:1)

We come to this, the final reflection on the theme of the work of God, the role of prayer and worship as a kind of liturgical theology. And it is fitting that we take the Lord's Prayer as the substance of this reflection. The disciple in Luke's account asked the Lord to "teach them to pray," a personal request for the good of the whole group. And lest we be tempted to feel wiser than the one who asked the Lord this boon, let us remember that, as Paul said, "We do not know how to pray as we ought, but [the] Spirit intercedes for us with sighs too deep for words" (Rom. 8:26).

Throughout these essays we have been looking at the church's collected sighs and groans—her prayers and her liturgies—as a means to come to a better understanding *of* God through acts of faith *in* God. The disciple asked Jesus to "teach them to pray," and I have been asking for God's grace, and I hope giving some guidance, as to how we might use the church's prayers and liturgies and "pray them to teach"—so to pray and worship that we might be taught, through that prayer and through that worship, some wisdom, some insight into the nature of God, faith seeking understanding through obedience to *lex orandi lex credendi*—the twin laws of belief and prayer. Even as hard-bitten a systematician as Karl Barth recognized that the work of theology cannot be accomplished apart from the work of prayer: "Because it has to be ever renewed, ever original, ever ready to be judged by God and God alone, theology must be an act of prayer" (167).

So in this reflection I propose to use "the prayer our Lord himself hath taught us" as a summary of what has been explored heretofore, but also as a brief *Summa* that encapsulates much of our Christian faith and mirrors the church's liturgical year, in a small compass.

But, you might well ask, why explore the Lord's Prayer as a statement of the faith rather than the Nicene Creed? The quick answer is to point out that this is simply turnabout: the doctrinal creed got added to our liturgy, so why not take our liturgical prayer and examine it for the doctrine it provides? But my real motives go deeper, deeper even than the simple facts of the Lord's Prayer's antiquity, dominical provenance, and universality, which all weigh heavily in its favor. But since the question of the creed has come up, it has to be acknowledged that there are problems with the creed, a statement of the faith, being used as a liturgical text, that are worth exploring before we head into a discussion of the Lord's Prayer. This will also serve in large part to summarize one of my major themes: the distinction between scholastic and liturgical theology.

When the church's leaders chose to insert the Nicene Creed into the liturgy, they were engaging in an essentially nonliturgical act. The late Episcopal scholar and liturgist Howard Galley used to joke that the creed came where it did in the liturgy so that after hearing a sermon of questionable theological soundness, the congregation could rise up and say, "Well, *we* believe in God. . . ." And the creed is in every sense just that: primarily a statement of belief somewhat miscast as an act of worship. The creation of the creed (in the fourth century) and its insertion into the liturgy (beginning in the fifth century) marked the commencement of the slow shift in the understanding of *orthodoxy* from "giving right glory" or "right worship" to "believing rightly."

The Nicene Creed was a creation born not of worship but of theological controversy, a litmus test to establish the bounds of heresy, the minimal constant teaching that could be signed up to on the dotted line. And so the Nicene Creed was somewhat uncomfortably plugged into our liturgy, originally as a weekly affirmation, but now, in large part due to the drift of meanings associated with the terms, as less a precise affirmation of a shared theology than a *communal* poke in the general direction of the faith to which one can attribute an astonishing range of *personal* meanings—or not, as the case may be. I recall a few years ago overhearing a Gen-X couple arguing at the coffee hour at an upscale Manhattan parish. They were visitors who had come primarily because of the parish's well-deserved musical reputation. The man asked the woman, "Do you really believe in the virgin birth?" She said, "Well, I'm not sure." He rejoined, "But you just *said* you did a few minutes ago back in there." "Oh. Oh, *well* . . ." she said, as if anything said "back in there" was relevant to anything one might think "out here."

When we say the creed, do we mean what we say or say what we mean, or know what we mean or say? And I'm not just talking about secularized Gen-X, Y, or Z-ers, but about those of us who, it can safely be assumed, take these matters seriously. For example, does the phrase "of one being" communicate the same meaning or bear the same weight to *our* ears as *homoousios* did to the Council of Nicea? What either phrase means is very difficult to explain—how the Son can be "of one *being* with" and yet not "be" the Father. Appeals to the classical distinctions between essence and existence, or *hypostasis* and *ousia*, are liable to draw blank looks in a world far removed from Plato and Aristotle. And no doubt "being" was substituted for the older translation "substance" because of the huge gap between the Nicene meaning of "substance" and what people mean today when they say that two things are "substantially the same"—that they are quite similar to each other but *not* the same—precisely the doctrine that the Council opposed.

Retreat back into the standby excuse, "It's a mystery," must evoke the question, "Then why say anything at all?" And of course, while the *academic theological* answer fumbles due to a lack of a shared philosophical worldview or metaphysic in which a meaning even of "being" can be agreed upon, the liturgical answer—I hasten to add not an *entirely* satisfactory one—is the strong feeling that the people need to have *something* to do. And since we have so clericalized the liturgy and told the laity they aren't "participating" unless they "do" something or "say" something, and since it is so much easier in our text-oriented mind-set to give them something to say, the Nicene Creed remains a ready-made solution to the perceived problem of a congregation with too much time on its hands.

Clearly the Nicene Creed as it stands in our liturgy today no longer serves as a precise doctrinal statement, but rather as a symbolic act of faith no better "understanded of" the bulk of the people than were the "hocus pocus" Latin liturgies of the High Middle Ages. While for theological sophisticates the creed may function as an asymptotic approximation to the incomprehensible, for the majority of the faithful it comprises simply their longest speech in the liturgical drama. But like the single long speech from the otherwise silent character Lucky in Samuel Beckett's *Waiting for Godot*, the *meaning* of the creed has become secondary to the *saying* of the creed. What is important now is not *what* the creed says, but *that* it is said, faith no longer seeking understanding, but content simply to say the right things—not so much (if at all) a statement of personal belief, but an affirmation that this is the text the church has said embodies the corporate faith of that church: faith *avoiding* any too precise an understanding; a wax nose pliable to any likeness, so long as it is said.

While saying a text in common is a liturgical act in itself—though not the most powerful—this particular recited formula we encounter week by week has become like the newsvendor from whom we buy our daily paper but whose name we do not know, and whose life beyond the confines of his newsstand is a total mystery. The church ought to take the time to explore the creed's significance beyond the merely verbal into the meaningful, unpacked through education *outside* of the liturgy, so that when it is recited *in* that liturgical context it might take on greater weight, of which familiarity and shifting meanings have robbed it.

However, as the creed is far too lengthy to unpack in this present context, what I would like to attempt here, by way of summary of our exploration thus far, is to look at the articles of the far shorter Lord's Prayer, to see if we may not find therein a more intimate and common faith, perhaps less tied up with the philosophical categories of Greek thought, and more immediately meaningful to us in the present day.

Now, I hasten to add that the Lord's Prayer, as a liturgical text, is no more immune to misunderstanding than any other text. *Recited* texts in particular tend to lose their meaning the more often they are recited—if the meaning was clear in the first place. I encountered an example of this when teaching a Sunday school class for the English-speaking children of the Spanish-speaking members of my Bronx parish. We were talking about the Lord's Prayer and had gotten to the phrase "deliver us from evil." I asked the class if any of them knew what this meant, and one charming little girl, a bright-eyed five-year-old, said, "We want God to take us away from the beach." I looked around at the other children, some of them as old as twelve, expecting them to giggle at this odd answer, but instead saw them all nodding grave assent to this proposition. I couldn't figure out where this idea might have come from, and how it had become so universally accepted as an article of faith by this juvenile council. All that leapt to my mind was Melina Mercouri's character in *Never on Sunday*, who thought that the Greek tragedy *Medea* ended with the family going off to the seashore.

Summoning my still-limited Spanish vocabulary, I said to the little girl, "But *beach* is *la playa*." She responded, with a patient schoolteacher's tone correcting my misunderstanding, "No, no. It's *libranos del mar*." That is, "Deliver us from *the sea!*" All these years the children had been hearing the soft terminal *L* of *del mal*, "from evil," as *del mar*—the phrase had suffered a sea-change, transformed into "from the sea." No one had ever taken the time to talk about the *meaning* of this text until that day, satisfied instead with teaching the mechanical repetition of syllables whose surmised meaning was subservient to their recitation, much like my own early experience of having been taught the Pater Noster in pre–Vatican II Sunday school—never told the meaning of this magic formula, only how to say the incantation.

That being said, I believe that the Lord's Prayer can serve us well in our liturgical-theological quest and provide a summary of what we have explored thus far. The style of this final meditation will allow us to ruminate on these words as we would in a prayer form only lightly touched on earlier: *lectio divina*. We will find that in the few scant words of this prayer we can explore in miniature a foundation on which to build our faith, and an echo of the church's liturgical year.

THE RELATIONAL GOD OF LOVE

Our Father

The very first word of this prayer (in English, anyway) casts us immediately into *community* and harks back to what was said about Pentecost in an earlier chapter. It neatly fits the disciple's request, "Teach *us* to pray," as a praying band of disciples. The prayer Jesus teaches that gathered group is not addressed simply to a transcendent vocative "*O* God," nor to the "*My* God" of personal piety, but to the supremely relational and related "*Our* God" of the church. *Our* is plural; it cannot exist without you and me, and it requires *both* you and me. Even when this prayer is prayed in solitude, it is addressed to the God who is *ours,* who is not simply the personal household God but the God of the church, the blessed company of all faithful people. Even when prayed in solitary silence, this prayer reminds us that we are not isolated, not alone.

And it also reminds us that we are not orphans. God is not simply *ours* but our *Father*. This immediately squares or triples the web of relationships. The Triune character of God is immediately manifest, as the Son addresses the Father in the Spirit of prayer and invites us into this relationship as children by adoption through our brother Jesus.

As explored in the chapter on images for God, and as countless mystics have shown us, the importance of the Fatherhood of God lies in God being parental, not paternal. The Fatherhood of God is not about gender, but generation and relationship. God is far more than the limiting definitions of the theologians who wished to see God as Pure Being, or Being Itself, or First Cause, or Unmoved Mover. "Father" reveals God to be God of relationship, God of love, God *in* relationship—not just eternally with the Son and Holy Spirit, but with us too, we who through Christ are bold enough to call God *our Father*, God who is the source of *our* life.

But since Jesus is speaking, including himself among us, this also links us in solidarity with him, Christ our older brother helping us to understand the tough lesson set for us in the Holy Trinity. For us to be invited by Jesus to join in calling God our Father is to assert the astounding truth: that we are, all of us, children of God through Jesus Christ. This was one of Jesus's most difficult teachings, and even today there are those who, wishing to preserve Christ's Johannine uniqueness as "the only Son of God," have lost sight of the astounding synoptic witness of the Lord's Prayer, the deeply scriptural teaching that Christ is not an only child but the firstborn of a large family (Rom. 8:29)—even if he is the *only-begotten* or *one-of-a-kind* son and we many siblings are all adopted. This goes back to the religious leaders' objection to what they saw as Jesus's claim to Sonship. In response, he cited Psalm 82:6 that affirms: "You are gods, children of the Most High, all of you" (John 10:34). The true uniqueness of Christ's sonship lay in his priority as firstborn, his role as the "beloved" begotten of the Father before all worlds; but it is precisely *as* the firstborn that it was and is his right to bring others into the family, welcoming and teaching us to call God our Father, our Abba, through the spirit of adoption (Rom. 8:15).

In heaven

So we pray to our Father in heaven, and the irreducible fact of our prayer directed to God affirms our hopeful belief that God exists. The human need to pray and the human experience of prayer assure us that we are not simply talking to ourselves. This is, of course, an assurance of faith, not certainty, of hope for what we do not see. But to echo Paul, if there were no God to hear our prayers, then we are of all people the most to be pitied (1 Cor. 15:19). Yet this is the human hope that joins the earthly trio along with faith and love to reflect the heavenly Trinity above.

The Lord's Prayer establishes the primary locus of God the Father in heaven, while affirming our connection with God through that opening possessive pronoun *our*. This allows us to preserve the distinction between the creator and the created, to affirm that God is intimately related to creation while at the same time subsisting outside of and apart from the creation. Heaven here is understood not simply as "what's up there," but as the realm of all possibilities and potentialities. Heaven in this sense is the realm of God's primordial nature, by which God is apart from any action or activity. And if we were to stop there, we would have the impassible God, the Unmoved Mover, the First Cause, of classical theology. But the Lord's Prayer does not allow us to stop there, because it didn't start there. It started with "Our Father"—beginning from *our* perspective, the perspective of the consequences of God's actions, of the radical actuality of *our* being and *our* praying, dealing with our apprehension of God here and now, before reminding us of God's primordial being there and then *in heaven*.

The first four words of this prayer establish a pattern that will be repeated throughout it: the relationship between the earthly and the heavenly, drawn in three bold lines, of which this is the first diagonal stroke connecting us with God—Our Father in heaven.

Worship and Ministry in the New Creation

There follow three imperatives relating to God, three commands, spoken as absolutely as God's own command at the beginning, "Let there be light!" We are in the realm of the imperative here, the "Let it be" not of passive toleration but of active and intentional creation.

Hallowed be your Name

"Hallowed be your Name" is a call to worship: not simply a statement or affirmation that "God's name is hallowed" but an imperative command that God's name is *to be hallowed*, to be worshiped and adored as *holy*. This command to worship is cast in the same mode as the ancient praise-shout *Hallelujah*—"Praise God"—which was addressed not only to the human world but to all of creation: the sun, moon, and stars, the planets in their courses, the mountains, the hills, and the trees, everything with and without breath praising God, whose name is Hallowed One.

This response, this worship, grows directly and immediately out of the first phrase that describes God and our relationship to God. The first fruit of awareness of this relationship is worship; the first human response to the presence of the Holy is a call to acknowledge and bless the name of the Holy One. The hallowing of that name is the substance of all worship, the bending of the knee that allows that which is hallowed to be seen to be above all, the bowing of the head and raising of the hand by which we acknowledge being in the presence of the Holy. We find ourselves back on holy ground along with Moses; only this time God's name is not the impatient "I am who I am," but the ever-loving and creative "Let there be," the name of Blessing. "Holy" is God's name: God's name *is* Hallowed, the Hallowed One, ever blessing, ever blessed.

Your kingdom come

"Your kingdom come" confronts us with the Advent theme with which our liturgical year begins: the fact that we live in the "not yet"—the creation not yet completed, in which the Father is still working. At the same time as we recognize our incomplete state, we call for completion, we shout our wish and hope for culmination. This ongoing dynamic, the creative tension between what is and what may be, is the place in which God acts, in the creative Now that is unfolding and becoming all around us, where we pray that what ought to be will become what is. In this phrase, "your kingdom come," and the next two, which call for God's will to be done on earth as it is in heaven, Jesus presents us with reality as an emergent process rather than as a fixed physicality, emphasizing the constantly ongoing nature of God at work in the world, and the world's subsistence in that ongoing process of God's being and revelation.

By way of analogy, think of music. The great composers hear music in their heads. Given their human limits, mortal composers can only hear so much music in their heads, so many possibilities limited by their culture, heritage, and the extent of their own genius. But imagine God for a moment as the source of all music, as the composer *par excellence*. In God's mind all of the various potential combinations of pitch and rhythm, the numberless sequences of notes and stacks of harmonies, coexist eternally and perfectly in one incredible chord. We might then understand the theological concept of Providence by way of this musical analogy: as God's gracious awareness and knowledge of all potentialities. If we then imagine that this world of ours, this cosmos, is the song that God is actually singing, from the beginning even up to this moment, we have found an active metaphor for the doctrine of Creation. The song in the mind of God is not yet complete, the kingdom has not yet come; and still it is unfolding all around us.

But where *is* the melody? Where, for that matter, is *any* melody? A song can only be said to exist in time as the relationship of each succeeding note to the one that went before and the one that comes after defines the identifiable melody. The *entity* of a song exists not as a *thing*, an *object* to which one can point, but rather as an *unfolding process of relationships*. And what I would suggest is that our world is much more like a song than we realize. We tend to think in terms of *things* rather than processes, of course, and this "essentialist" way of seeing the world seems to have some good common sense to it, at least when you are talking about inanimate objects. But when we come to living things, the matter clearly becomes more complicated.

Ask yourself this question: who am I? We've all said, "I'm not what I was ten years ago," without realizing that it is literally true: the matter that makes up my body is constantly being replaced as I eat and breathe. Yet there is far more to me than the matter that makes up my body at any given moment. So what am I?

It seems that what I "am" is the moment-by-moment interrelationship of many particles and energies, not always the same, unified by some sense of identity that endures over time, apprehended from my past actuality and pointed toward my future potentiality. In short, I am a process, more a doing than a being, more a song than a sculpture—like an identifiable realm that endures even with the change in monarch or subjects.

Moreover, my personal realm doesn't have a hard boundary. At an atomic level there is a constant interchange between "me" and my surroundings, and both my influence and what influences me extend far beyond the limits of my skin. Physically speaking, every particle in the universe, including those that make up me or you, exercises some minute gravitational force on every other particle in the universe, however distant or however minuscule. And who knows what other forces may be at work when we move to the levels of the conscious mind or the spirit? We are not closed-off monads of existence, but a whole chorus of voices echoing through time and space. As you read these words in this present moment, I can be said to have prompted changes in you through them, from my vantage as I write them, months or years ago from the moment in which you read them. As you read these very words, chemicals are being released in your brain, small physical and electrochemical pulses are reverberating, ideas are forming, physically changing you *now* at a microscopic level yet billowing up in waves to form thoughts at a perceptible level. So I might say that there's a little bit of "me" in "you" now, synapses connected in ways they never would have been had you not read these words. You will never be the same again—that possibility has perished as many new ones (based on the new you) have emerged.

And what we have accomplished in this—me in writing and you in reading—in a very small way, evoking tiny changes in your mental state, simply giving you something to think about, God is doing in a huge way to everything, to you and to me in our totality as entities (not just what we say or think but how we are and what we become) as the kingdom of God unfolds, not yet complete, but coming into being all around us. God is singing the melody to which the universe is dancing. And as God sings this song of the universe, God is also the mind and heart that knows and hears the whole tune that we only experience in part. God's heart is storing up the treasured melody even as the transitory notes pass out of existence, so that in God's kingdom, when it comes, the song may be sung forever; and so we pray for God's Advent: "your kingdom come."

Now, we might well ask, just what is this "kingdom" whose coming we urge and seek? Keeping in mind Jesus's advice about the coin bearing the image and likeness of Caesar, the contrast between any earthly kingdom and God's kingdom stands out like a coal on a snowbank. If we want to know the character of the divine kingdom whose coming is the focus of our hopes, we will find those hopes reflected in the divine desire fulfilled in Christ, and in his words, especially as recorded in Matthew's Gospel.

This kingdom is like a mustard seed which, when planted, grows not into a mustard plant but into a tree that can support the nests of literally heavenly birds (*peteina tou ouranou*); it is like leaven which cannot be hidden (literally *encrypted*) in flour, but which makes its presence known by its effervescent expansion (13:32–33). This is a kingdom that is unexpected and unmistakable, whose coming lights up the skies from one end to the other (24:27).

Yet this kingdom is also a kingdom of judgment and justice, of discernment and decision. The rule of this kingdom separates wheat from chaff and weeds (3:12; 13:40), good fish from bad (13:48), sheep from goats (25:33), and one wedding guest from another (22:13). Finally, although we bid this kingdom come, Jesus also assures us it is near—carried and present with the disciples in their apostolic work of spreading the good news (10:7) and promised to some of them even before their death (16:28); and adding Luke's testimony, "among you" (17:21).

These are the characteristics of the kingdom of God, already but not yet among us, as we daily pray in Advent expectation that it "come."

Your will be done

Naturally we hope and pray that the actuality coming into being day by day and then passing eternally into the heart of God will reflect the *will* of God, this will that we pray "be done." And yet we understand that the will of God, providential and gracious as it is, is not coercive. The universe is free even while constrained by the laws of nature. But as the quantum physicists are telling us these days, even the laws of nature are not so constrained as once we thought they were and randomness lies at the smallest scales. And so, if I can switch my analogy from the musical to the visual arts, the will of God is not the mechanical reproduction of a rubber stamp, but the creative will of a free brushstroke. Painters refer to the *tooth* of the medium upon which they paint, whether canvas or paper or gessoed board. This *tooth* is the resistance and texture that gives interest to the brushstroke, gently resisting the movement of the brush, yet by that very resistance combined with the artist's skill producing the serendipitous final effect.

In the gift of free will to humanity, God has introduced a large measure of *tooth* into the universal canvas. I leave aside here the question of how much that freedom is based at root on some quantum necessity for randomness, or the extent to which other creatures share in the emerging qualities of that freedom. But I am secure in thinking that our human will tempers God's will for us, resistant or pliant, providing the ground for new possibilities for grace even in our refusals to do God's will. We are free to do many things which we know full well to be contrary to God's will, and yet we know that God the master artist can make the most felicitous use of even our gravest culpabilities—that the stone which the builder rejected can become the keystone of the corner.

We pray, "Your will be done," as Jesus our *Lord* taught us; but we are reminded that this is the prayer that Jesus our *brother* prayed himself as he knelt in dark Gethsemane. And it is in the passion of Christ that we see the awesome mystery of God's will being done, even when all the forces of evil seem to be set against God. Saint Francis de Sales spoke of *two* wills of God: God's original will and what he called "God's good will done." God's original will and intent for humankind is always good. But human freedom kicks against the goad. Human building-stones are uneven and misshapen. Human freedom crucifies the Son of God. Still God is able to take these misshapen stones and batter them into shape for the head of the corner. God is able to take the most perverse twistings of human wrong and somehow weave them back into the tapestry of God's good will done. God is able to take the instrument of shameful death and make it into the source of life. God, in Christ, can transform the human freedom that crucified him, through human obedience, into the salvation of the world—and God's good will done. God's unchanging will for good accommodated our wrongs and brought about the greatest good in spite of the greatest wrong, the redemption of the world through the passion and death of Jesus Christ. And so we pray, in hope for the future based on trust from the past, "Your will be done."

Within this Advent portion of the prayer, we have invoked a trinity of Name, Realm, and Will—affirmed in imperatives to be hallowed, coming, and accomplished. This is no substitute for the Triune Name, yet it stands beside it as a kind of economic expression of Godhead: it bears the authority of the selfsame dominical source, and it reveals the character of God in action, responsive to our prayer. It will find an echo in the closing doxology added to the Lord's words in liturgical worship: for God's is the kingdom, power, and glory, whose Name is Holy, whose Kingdom comes, whose Will is done.

On earth as in heaven

"On earth as in heaven"—thus we find ourselves completing the second stroke, the second diagonal line connecting the here and now of earth with the there and then of heaven. But while the first stroke begins with us and ends with the Father in heaven, this stroke starts with God's will in heaven and ends on earth, where we pray God's will be done as it is above.

There has always been a strong desire among human beings to replicate heaven upon earth. Acknowledging the poverty of our efforts, one of the most enduring ways in which human beings have attempted to capture the feeling of heaven on earth is in the art of architecture. As we saw in an earlier chapter, this is a fairly universal religious impulse, not limited to Christianity. The tabernacle of the desert, the temple of Solomon, and the visionary temple of Ezekiel all were purported to have been earthly replicas of God's dwelling in heaven. The imperial palace of China was designed to reflect the administrative hierarchy of Heaven. And we are well familiar with the Moorish earthly paradises of Granada, the Alhambra, and Topkapi. There is a deeply human desire to recreate in miniature down here, however imperfectly, that heavenly reality we know exists "up there."

Even God appears to be in on this kind of creative miniaturization. The creation account in the first chapter of Genesis can be read as an analogy to the construction of an ancient near-eastern temple. You have the foundation and walls of the structure, the roof, the pool for the lustral water, then the lampstands, the decorative borders portraying vegetation and living creatures. Then finally, in the most holy place, the image of the God who is worshiped. Thus all of the physical world is a temple built by God for the worship of God, and the image God placed in the Holiest Place is the image of God: the *humanum*.

This architecture is recapitulated in the Incarnation, in the Word made flesh. All our long journey from the Fall until now has been the effort, aided by God's Spirit and completed and revealed in the fullness of time by the Incarnation of God's Son, to restore that fallen temple. And this was not by force: the assent of humanity was required. Here in the person of the Virgin Mary of Nazareth, humanity consents to the will of God being done on earth as it is in heaven, and of her substance the temple not built with hands, the temple of Christ's body, is constructed. And so we say, moving on in our miniature liturgical year to Christmastide and the Epiphany: your will be done, on earth as it is in heaven.

Give us today our daily bread

We have entered into the Holy of Holies, the place where the image of God dwells. And we ask God to give us our daily bread. This is the first clause in the Lord's Prayer that could be called an ordinary petition. Up until now, everything we've asked for has been universal, directed to God and the nature of God. The first thing we have asked for *us* is daily bread. And it is for *us*—not just for me, my own needs, my own hunger—this is *ours*. This is the bread of a common humanity, shared in a common meal. As the great Dominican preacher Meister Eckhart noted in *his* commentary on the Lord's Prayer, "There is no such thing as *my* bread." This center of the prayer is the place where all the lines meet: we have come from talk of earth and heaven on earth, and hence will move to sin and forgiveness. But here, where X marks the spot, here in this center of the prayer we sit down at table with our Lord and share in the breaking of the bread; God truly has set a table for *us* in the midst of things, in the midst of our gathering.

The *daily* of this bread has long been associated with the custom of daily Eucharist, of the whenever-you-do-thisness of the act of remembrance, of re-membering the body. It is also long-connected with the daily manna of the wilderness, sufficient to the day, except on the Sabbath when an extra day's ration was included. The dailyness of this bread reminds us yet again of the way in which God works, moment by moment, day by day, in the green season of our ordinary time, full of epiphanies to remind us to re-member God. This is the quantum nature of life, the quantum nature of how God works, providing bread sufficient for the day each day. We are given, in short, just as much reality as we can handle, daily rations for our daily life. "One day at a time" may well have been adopted as a slogan by Alcoholics Anonymous, but the truth that this is how God's world works goes back to the beginning.

This petition also expresses our hunger, our hunger not just for daily bread but for every word that proceeds from the mouth of the Most High. This petition—"Give!"—expresses the wound of separation, the hunger that has afflicted us from the time our ancient progenitor was cast out of the garden of unearned fruit for the fault of taking forbidden fruit, and made to till the soil and gain, by the sweat of the brow, what fruit it might grudgingly bear, what scattered grain that human skill might craft into bread. And yet, once again, how like God to take that cursed bread and transform it into the vehicle of God's presence with us, in word and sacrament, to take the bread of punishment and make it the gift not just of daily life, but of eternal life. And so our hunger, our deepest hunger, is relieved day by day with enough for each day, as we come to know God-with-us in the breaking of the bread.

SIN AND REDEMPTION

The final petitions and the closing doxology of the Lord's Prayer mark the third stroke, a strong vertical line connecting heaven and earth, completing an emblem like an asterisk, reminiscent of the Chi-Rho, the early monogram of our Lord, the sign in which Constantine found victory.

Forgive us our sins

And we begin this stroke in the depths with the acknowledgment of our sins and an appeal for forgiveness, as we adopt the Lenten theme of penitence. The hunger for our daily bread has reminded us of why we have that hunger. This petition introduces explicitly the notion that all is not right with the world. The world is not simply incomplete; it is broken. Something is wrong, and we are responsible. There is no suggestion that this cry for forgiveness is an optional clause that can be left out when we are tempted to play the role of Pharisee instead of Publican. Jesus knew who he was teaching how to pray, and he knew that just as we hunger for daily bread, so too we daily repeat those actions of selfishness and pride that led to the need for earthly bread in the first place. Just as we need daily bread, we need daily to be forgiven, not just seven times to fill out the week, but seventy times seven, and more.

As we forgive those who sin against us

Yet as hard as it may seem that we cannot omit the acknowledgment of our sins, as we come to the next clause of the prayer we rejoice to find that there is a way out—to forgive those who sin against us. And this out-clause seems at first to offer a solution so simple that we are likely to say, "It's a snap." But forgiving isn't that easy, even though it is the only way to be forgiven. We cannot undo our own sins, we can only be forgiven them—and forgiveness always lies with those who have been wounded by our sin. And as we all have sinned and been sinned against, wounding and wounded, we can begin—we must begin—by forgiving the sins done against *us*, robbing them of their effect, neutralizing their poison with forgiveness, allowing the wounds that others have dealt us to heal—as only we can: for whatever medicine or therapy may be applied to the wounded body, it is ultimately the body itself that must heal. If we would rather pick at our wounds and injuries and worry them, they will never heal; but if we forgive those who inflicted them, the healing will begin.

This is why Christ's redeeming act, and his words of forgiveness from the cross, why his Passiontide echoes so resoundingly through the central words of this prayer. Human sin brought about not only the wounding of the world, but the wounding and the death of the world's maker. And Christ's forgiveness of the greatest sin imaginable, and his return to life again, still bearing those wounds and yet forgiving not only those who inflicted them, but those who abandoned him because of them, opens for us a way of healing through forgiveness. Julian of Norwich saw room for all who were to be saved precisely in the wound in Jesus's side, when he said not "Look what you've done!" but "See how I loved you" (24).

And so arrayed for Lent and Passiontide, we pray our public and general confession that we may be forgiven, even and only as we forgive.

Save us from the time of trial

"Save us from the time of trial" is one of the more difficult verses of this prayer, for textual reasons. The old version reads, "Lead us not into temptation," which sounds like a very different thing. Perhaps "save us *in* the time of trial" or "save us *through* the time of trial" would be a bit more harmonious and capture the sense more effectively.

What *is* the trial—what is the temptation from or through which we wish to be saved, into which we do not wish to be led? Hunger and the knowledge of our sin has turned this prayer in a rather scary direction, suitable to Lent and Holy Week. And perhaps the time of trial, the temptation, is simply that awakened knowledge of our daily tendency to veer off the heavenward track into the ruts and gutters of sin and wrong, the hard, dry wasteland of unforgiving hearts, the breadless desert of self, or the constant worry that what is sufficient for one day will run out—and who can trust there will be more? For the trial is the one for which we all have a court date: the final judgment in which we will stand at the last: and will we indeed see our Redeemer on our side? This petition is a plea for acquittal when we stand in that court, when we face the unblinking eye of the one who has known us all along and through and through. This is a character witness who knows our character fully—and will he speak for the defense? That is our earnest plea; perhaps our earnest plea bargain, since we know we are guilty.

And deliver us from evil

So our Lord prompts us to call out "and deliver us from evil." This is our own acknowledged evil, which we confess, as well as the externally personified "evil one"—the prosecuting attorney who stands to accuse us in the time of trial, as if our own sins did not speak loudly enough against us. The time of trial, the temptation, and the evil from which we seek deliverance is that sin-sickened, wounded, and debilitated existence, sentenced to the prison of the unforgiving and unforgiven self, besieged by grace but starving inwardly, starved of the rich potentiality that grace offers, by our insistent determination on our own way. We are truly in the very depths here, lost in the dark, stumbling, wounded, starving, and dying. It is the hour of stillness after the deposition from the cross, the breadless Sabbath of a Holy Saturday, when even the angels hold their breath.

For the kingdom, the power, and the glory are yours, now and forever

And yet... and yet even at the grave we make our song, alleluia, alleluia, alleluia. Even from the depths of the grave, even from the depths of trial, temptation, and evil, we raise our eyes to look to the hills from whence cometh our help and proclaim our Easter faith: for the kingdom and the power and the glory are God's, now and forever. And the final stroke of this prayer, of this great Chi-Rho, having begun in the depths of sin and death suddenly leaps to the heights, from the depth of confession of sin to the heights of confession of faith, to that place beyond all time and space where the Trinity dwells in all majesty, with all power, in all glory.

The prayer that Jesus taught lacked this glorious doxology. It was added by the early church as an affirmation that in spite of evil and through the victory of the cross, Christ is risen and reigns in glory, seated at God's right hand. This closing clause is the resurrection appearance that follows on the discovery of the empty tomb, the exclamation point that gestures upward to where Christ has ascended to prepare a way for us in a perpetual Eastertide. So we end this prayer in that affirmation, an affirmation of faith, with all being and doing, all existence and strength and glory in God's hands. Christ is risen indeed.

CONCLUSION

This is the prayer our Savior taught us. This is the pattern of all our prayer. May we so pray this and all our prayers, all our liturgies, and all our worship; may we so carry aloft the emblem of Christ, the Chi-Rho of our worship, the sign in which we find our victory, lifting high the cross, all the days of our life until we come to that heavenly kingdom where we shall know as we are known, and love as we are loved, and worship forever in the liturgy of heaven, as we contemplate our God, in endless bliss.

Soli Deo Gloria

This Victorious Sign

References and Acknowledgments

This book has no footnotes. Modern sources appear below and are referenced in the text as follows: when context makes clear the work referred to, a number will indicate the page. In the case of classic literature, the number indicates the section of the work, using traditional numeration. Otherwise the author's name (and publication year if more than one work is referenced) followed by a page or section number will suffice. A few additional titles are included for further reading.

References

Anson, Peter F. *Churches: Their Plan and Furnishing.* Milwaukee: Bruce, 1948.

———. *Fashions in Church Furnishings: 1840–1940.* 2nd ed. London: Studio Vista Ltd., 1965.

Barth, Karl. *Evangelical Theology.* Grand Rapids, MI: William B. Eerdmans, 1963.

Bass, Diana Butler. *The Practicing Congregation.* Washington, DC: Alban Institute, 2004.

Baxter, Richard. *The Practical Works.* Vol. 23. London: James Duncan, 1830.

Bouyer, Louis. *Rite & Man: Natural Sacredness and Christian Liturgy.* Notre Dame, IN: University of Notre Dame Press, 1963.

Chauvet, Louis-Marie. *Symbol and Sacrament.* New York: Pueblo, 1995.

Congregation for Divine Worship and Discipline of the Sacraments. "Praying Ad Orientem Versus." *Notitiae* 332, vol. 29, no. 5 (May 1993): 245–49.

Dolnick, Edward. *The Seeds of Life.* New York: Basic Books, 2017.

Fischer, Balthasar. *Signs, Words and Gestures.* New York: Pueblo, 1981.
Francis of Assisi. "Second Version of the Letter to the Faithful." In *Francis and Clare: The Complete Works.* New York: Paulist Press, 1982.
Gamber, Klaus. *Reform of the Roman Liturgy: Its Problems and Background.* San Juan Capistrano: Una Voce Press, 1993.
Guiver, George, *Company of Voices: Daily Prayer and the People of God.* New York: Pueblo, 1988.
Hammond, Peter. *Liturgy and Architecture.* New York: Columbia University Press, 1961.
Julian of Norwich. *Shewings* or *Revelations of Divine Love.* My translation of the Middle English. Reference numbers refer to the chapter of the Long Text.
Jungmann, Josef A., S.J. *The Early Liturgy.* Notre Dame, IN: University of Notre Dame Press, 1959.
Kavanagh, Aidan. *On Liturgical Theology.* Collegeville, MN: Liturgical Press, 1984.
Kevern, John R. "The Ecclesiology of the Concordat," *The Anglican* 25, no. 1 (July 1996).
Lewis, C.S. *The Four Loves.* New York: Harcourt Brace Jovanovich, Inc., 1960.

———. *Letters to Malcolm: Chiefly on Prayer.* New York: Harcourt Brace Jovanovich, Inc., 1964.
Lowrie, Walter. *Action in the Liturgy.* New York: Philosophical Library, 1953.
McGarvey, William. *Liturgiae Americanae.* Philadelphia: Philadelphia Church, 1907.
Procter-Smith, Marjorie. "Images of Women in the Lectionary," *Concilium* 182. Edinburgh: T&T Clark, 1985.
Ratzinger, Josef. *Spirit of the Liturgy.* San Francisco: Ignatius Press, 2000.
Sacred Congregation for the Doctrine of the Faith. *Inter Insigniores: Declaration . . . on the question of admission of women to the ministerial priesthood, 1976.* In *Women Priests: Obstacle to Unity?* London: Catholic Truth Society, 1986.
Simmons, David, ObJN. *The Julian Parish Missal.* Available online at www.julianparishmissal.org.

Spencer, Bonnell, OHC. *Sacrifice of Thanksgiving.* West Park, NY: Holy Cross Publications, 1965.

Suchocki, Marjorie Hewitt. *In God's Presence: Theological Reflections on Prayer.* St. Louis, MO: Chalice Press, 1996.

Tillich, Paul. "Nature and Sacrament." In *Paul Tillich: Theologian of the Boundaries,* edited by Mark Kline Taylor. Minneapolis: Fortress Press, 1991.

Underhill, Evelyn. *Worship.* New York: Harper & Brothers, 1937.

Yokarinis, Constantine. "A Patristic Basis for a Theological Anthropology of Women in Their Distinctive Humanity," *The Anglican Theological Review* 84, no. 3 (Summer 2002).

Acknowledgments

I want to thank Nancy Bryan and the publishers for their kindness and patience in bringing this project to fruition; but I must first thank Fr. John-Julian Swanson, OJN, for the invitation to lead his community's long retreat in 2001 that led to the substance of some of these reflections; and Peter S. Hawkins, whose account of his meeting with Canon West has remained vivid in my memory all these years. I am eternally grateful to the members of the Brotherhood of Saint Gregory, in particular its founder, Richard Thomas Biernacki, without whose inspiration I would not be who or where I am today. I also thank Thomas Bushnell, in particular for his conversation over some philosophical nitty-gritty; and James Teets, who has shared this journey with me for well over half of my earthly life. And finally, as I must always say as a good Gregorian, to God alone be the glory.

www.ingramcontent.com/pod-product-compliance
Ingram Content Group UK Ltd.
Pitfield, Milton Keynes, MK11 3LW, UK
UKHW021841140426
5217IPUK00022B/1540